CBEST STUDY GUIDE 2016

Test Preparation and Practice Test Questions for the
CBEST Exam

TABLE OF CONTENTS

INTRODUCTION

Congratulations on your decision to join the field of teaching—few other professions are so rewarding! By purchasing this book, you've already taken the first step towards succeeding in your career. The next step is to do well on the CBEST exam, which will require you to demonstrate knowledge of high-school level reading, writing, math, and science.

This book will walk you through the important concepts in each of these subjects and also provide you with inside information on test strategies and tactics. Even if it's been years since you graduated from high school or cracked open a textbook, don't worry—this book contains everything you'll need for the CBEST.

ABOUT TRIVIUM TEST PREP

Trivium Test Prep uses industry professionals with decades' worth of knowledge in their fields, proven with degrees and honors in law, medicine, business, education, the military, and more, to produce high-quality test prep books for students.

Our study guides are specifically designed to increase any student's score, regardless of his or her current skill level. Our books are also shorter and more concise than typical study guides, so you can increase your score while significantly decreasing your study time.

HOW TO USE THIS GUIDE

This guide is not meant to waste your time on superfluous information or concepts you've already learned. Instead, we hope you use this guide to focus on the concepts YOU need to master for the test and to develop critical test-taking skills. To support this effort, the guide provides:

- organized concepts with detailed explanations
- practice questions with worked-through solutions
- key test-taking strategies
- simulated one-on-one tutor experience
- tips, tricks, and test secrets

Because we have eliminated "filler" or "fluff," you'll be able to work through the guide at a significantly faster pace than you would with other test prep books. By allowing you to focus only on those concepts that will increase your score, we'll make your study time shorter and more effective.

WHAT IS THE CBEST?

The California Basic Educational Skills Test (CBEST) is a three-section exam (Math, Reading, and Writing) that is used by the states of California and Oregon to assess the knowledge of those wishing to become teachers, instructors, administrators, or personnel specialists.

The CBEST is created and administered by National Evaluation Systems, Inc. To register for the exam and find testing locations, visit the NES at www.ctcexams.nesinc.com.

WHAT'S ON THE CBEST?

The CBEST is a computer-based test that includes three sections with a total of one hundred multiple choice questions and two essays.

- The reading section includes 50 multiple-choice questions that are based on information provided in a short passage, table, or graph. Each passage is typically only 100-200 words in length. The questions require no additional or outside information, meaning the answer can always be derived from the provided information.
- The math section includes 50 multiple-choice questions, which cover estimation, measurement, statistics, and basic algebra. You may not use a calculator on this section.
- The writing section will require you to write two essays, one expository and one expressive.

You have four hours to take the test and may move between the sections at your own pace. Timing yourself can help take the pressure off while you work, but it also means you need to keep an eye on the clock. As you take practice tests, make a note of how long each section takes so you can leave yourself enough time for each section on the real test.

Before the test, you'll be given a fifteen minute tutorial on how to use the computer program. Once the timed test starts, you may take breaks, but they will be considered part of your allowed four hours.

HOW IS THE CBEST SCORED?

You'll receive a single point for each multiple choice question you answer correctly; you will not lose any points for questions answered incorrectly. Each essay is scored by four professional graders from 1 to 4 for a total score between 4 and 16. The raw scores for each section are then scaled to give a score between 20 and 80. Thus, for the range of scaled scores for the entire test is 60 – 240.

To pass the exam, you must earn a combined score of 123 for the Reading, Mathematics, and Writing; that's an average of 41 on each section. However, to pass you must score at least a 37 on each individual section regardless of your total score.

STRATEGIES FOR MULTIPLE CHOICE TESTING

1. Read all the answer choices. There will often be incorrect answers that seem correct at first glance (usually put there on purpose by test makers). If you go with the first answer you see that looks right, you might miss the better answer just a little bit further down the page.

2. Know the instructions and rules before taking the test. If you know exactly what you need to do and how long you have to answer each question, you don't have to waste time reading instruction.

3. Learn your pace. If you know how long each section of the test usually takes you to finish, you can avoid the problem of leaving questions unanswered when time runs out.

4. Think positive. Test makers rarely make the correct answer a negative statement that disparages or degrades someone or something.

5. Studying is a marathon, not a sprint. Don't try to cram all your study time in at once, and certainly don't start studying the day before the test.

6. Double check your answers. If you're taking a pencil-and-paper test, you'll want to be sure you're bubbling in for the correct question. If you're taking a computer test, you might not have the chance to go back and check your answer later.

WE WANT TO HEAR FROM YOU

Here at Trivium Test Prep our hope is that we not only taught you the relevant information needed to pass the exam, but that we helped you exceed all previous expectations. Our goal is to keep our guides concise, show you a few test tricks along the way, and ultimately help you succeed in your goals.

On that note, we are always interested in your feedback. To let us know if we've truly prepared you for the exam, please email us at feedback@triviumtestprep.com. Feel free to include your test score!

Your success is our success. Good luck on the exam and your future ventures.

Sincerely,

-Trivium Test Prep Team-

PART I: MATHEMATICS

THE MOST COMMON MISTAKES

The mathematics section of the CBEST includes fifty multiple choice questions that cover topics including measurement, simple algebra, basic statistics, and operations like addition and multiplication. You'll see problems that ask you to:

- Manipulate standard units.
- Perform basic operations such as addition, subtraction, multiplication, and division.
- Perform basic operations with fractions and decimals.
- Calculate percentages.
- Solve algebraic equations.
- Compare numbers.
- Interpret and find data on graphs and tables.
- Find basic statistical values such as mean, median, mode, and percentile.
- Calculate probabilities.

STRATEGIES FOR THE MATHEMATICS SECTION

Go Back to the Basics

First and foremost, practice your basic skills: sign changes, order of operations, simplifying fractions, and equation manipulation. These are the skills used most on the CBEST, though they are applied in different contexts. Remember that when it comes down to it, all math problems rely on the four basic skills of addition, subtraction, multiplication, and division. All you need to figure out is the order in which they're used to solve a problem.

Don't Rely on Mental Math

Using mental math is great for eliminating answer choices, but ALWAYS WRITE DOWN YOUR WORK! This cannot be stressed enough. Use whatever paper is provided; by writing and/or drawing out the problem, you are more likely to catch any mistakes. The act of writing things down also forces you to organize your calculations, leading to an improvement in your CBEST score.

The Three-Times Rule

You should read each question at least three times to ensure you're using the correct information and answering the right question:

Step One: Read the question and write out the given information.

Step Two: Read the question, set up your equation(s), and solve.

Step Three: Read the question and check that your answer makes sense (is the amount too large or small; is the answer in the correct unit of measure, etc.).

Make an Educated Guess

Eliminate those answer choices which you are relatively sure are incorrect, and then guess from the remaining choices. Educated guessing is critical to increasing your score.

NUMBERS AND OPERATIONS

I n order to do any type of math—whether it's basic geometry or advanced calculus—you need to have a solid understanding of numbers and operations. The specific operations the CBEST will test you on are covered in this chapter.

WORKING WITH POSITIVE & NEGATIVE NUMBERS

Adding, multiplying, and dividing numbers can yield positive or negative values depending on the signs of the original numbers. Knowing these rules can help determine if your answer is correct.

$(+) + (-)$ = the sign of the larger number

$(-) + (-)$ = negative number

$(-) \times (-)$ = positive number

$(-) \times (+)$ = negative number

$(-) \div (-)$ = positive number

$(-) \div (+)$ = negative number

Examples

Find the product of −10 and 47.

$(-) \times (+) = (-)$

$-10 \times 47 = \mathbf{-470}$

What is the sum of −65 and −32?

$(-) + (-) = (-)$

$-65 + -32 = \mathbf{-97}$

ORDER OF OPERATIONS

Operations in a mathematical expression are always performed in a specific order, which is described by the acronym PEMDAS:

1. Parentheses
2. Exponents
3. Multiplication
4. Division
5. Addition
6. Subtraction

Perform the operations within parentheses first, and then address any exponents. After those steps, perform all multiplication and division. These are carried out from left to right as they appear in the problem.

Finally, do all required addition and subtraction, also from left to right as each operation appears in the problem.

Examples

Solve: $[-(2)^2 - (4 + 7)]$

First, complete operations within parentheses:

$-(2)^2 - (11)$

Second, calculate the value of exponential numbers:

$-(4) - (11)$

Finally, do addition and subtraction:

$-4 - 11 = $ **−15**

Solve: $(5)^2 \div 5 + 4 \times 2$

First, calculate the value of exponential numbers:

$(25) \div 5 + 4 \times 2$

Second, calculate division and multiplication from left to right:

$5 + 8$

Finally, do addition and subtraction:

$5 + 8 = $ **13**

Solve the expression: $15 \times (4 + 8) - 3^3$

First, complete operations within parentheses:

$15 \times (12) - 3^3$

Second, calculate the value of exponential numbers:

$15 \times (12) - 27$

Third, calculate division and multiplication from left to right:

$180 - 27$

Finally, do addition and subtraction from left to right:

$180 - 27 = \mathbf{153}$

Solve the expression: $\left(\frac{5}{2} \times 4\right) + 23 - 4^2$

First, complete operations within parentheses:

$(10) + 23 - 4^2$

Second, calculate the value of exponential numbers:

$(10) + 23 - 16$

Finally, do addition and subtraction from left to right:

$(10) + 23 - 16$

$33 - 16 = \mathbf{17}$

UNITS OF MEASUREMENT

You are expected to memorize some units of measurement. These are given below. When doing unit conversion problems (i.e., when converting one unit to another), find the conversion factor, then apply that factor to the given measurement to find the new units.

Table 1.1. Unit Prefixes

PREFIX	SYMBOL	MULTIPLICATION FACTOR
tera	T	1,000,000,000,000
giga	G	1,000,000,000
mega	M	1,000,000
kilo	k	1,000
hecto	h	100
deca	da	10
base unit	--	--
deci	d	0.1
centi	c	0.01
milli	m	0.001
micro	μ	0.0000001
nano	n	0.0000000001
pico	p	0.0000000000001

Table 1.2. Units and Conversion Factors

DIMENSION	AMERICAN	SI
length	inch/foot/yard/mile	meter
mass	ounce/pound/ton	gram
volume	cup/pint/quart/gallon	liter
force	pound-force	newton
pressure	pound-force per square inch	pascal
work and energy	cal/British thermal unit	joule
temperature	Fahrenheit	kelvin
charge	faraday	coulomb

CONVERSION FACTORS

1 in = 2.54 cm	1 lb = 0.454 kg
1 yd = 0.914 m	1 cal = 4.19 J
1 mile = 1.61 km	1 °F = 5/9 (°F − 32)
1 gallon = 3.785 L	1 cm3 = 1 mL
1 oz = 28.35 g	1 hour = 3600 s

You'll be given conversion factors if they're needed for a problems, but it's still good to familiarize yourself with common ones before the test.

Examples

A fence measures 15 ft. long. How many yards long is the fence?

1 yd. = 3 ft.

$\frac{15}{3}$ = **5 yd.**

A pitcher can hold 24 cups. How many gallons can it hold?

1 gal. = 16 cups

$\frac{24}{16}$ = **1.5 gallons**

A spool of wire holds 144 in. of wire. If Mario has 3 spools, how many feet of wire does he have?

12 in. = 1 ft.

$\frac{144}{12}$ = 12 ft.

12 ft. × 3 spools = **36 ft. of wire**

How many millimeters are in 0.5 m?

1 meter = 1000 mm

0.5 meters = **500 mm**

A lead ball weighs 38 g. How many kilograms does it weigh?

1 kg = 1000 g

$\frac{38}{1000}$ g = **0.038 kg**

How many cubic centimeters are in 10 L?

   1 L = 1000

   10 L = 1000 × 10

   10 L = **10,000**

Jennifer's pencil was initially 10 centimeters long. After she sharpened it, the pencil was 9.6 centimeters long. How many millimeters did she lose from her pencil by sharpening it?

   1 cm = 10 mm

   10 cm – 9.6 cm = 0.4 cm lost

   0.4 cm = 10 × .4 mm = **4 mm were lost**

DECIMALS AND FRACTIONS

Adding and Subtracting Decimals

When adding and subtracting decimals, line up the numbers so that the decimals are aligned. You want to subtract the ones place from the ones place, the tenths place from the tenths place, etc.

Examples

Find the sum of 17.07 and 2.52.

   17.07

   + 2.52

   = **19.59**

Jeannette has 7.4 gallons of gas in her tank. After driving, she has 6.8 gallons How many gallons of gas did she use?

   7.4

   – 6.8

   = **0.6 gal.**

Multiplying and Dividing Decimals

When multiplying decimals, start by multiplying the numbers normally. You can then determine the placement of the decimal point in the result by adding the number of digits after the decimal in each of the numbers you multiplied together.

When dividing decimals, you should move the decimal point in the divisor (the number you're dividing by) until it is a whole. You can then move the decimal in the dividend (the number you're dividing into) the same number of places in the same direction. Finally, divide the new numbers normally to get the correct answer.

CONTINUE

Examples

What is the product of 0.25 and 1.4?

> $25 \times 14 = 350$
>
> There are 2 digits after the decimal in 0.25 and one digit after the decimal in 1.4. Therefore the product should have 3 digits after the decimal: **0.350** is the correct answer.

Find $0.8 \div 0.2$.

> Change 0.2 to 2 by moving the decimal one space to the right.
>
> Next, move the decimal one space to the right on the dividend. 0.8 becomes 8.
>
> Now, divide 8 by 2.
>
> $8 \div 2 = \mathbf{4}$

Find the quotient when 40 is divided by 0.25.

> First, change the divisor to a whole number: 0.25 becomes 25.
>
> Next, change the dividend to match the divisor by moving the decimal two spaces to the right, so 40 becomes 4000.
>
> Now divide: $4000 \div 25 = \mathbf{160}$

Working with Fractions

FRACTIONS are made up of two parts: the NUMERATOR, which appears above the bar, and the DENOMINATOR, which is below it. If a fraction is in its SIMPLEST FORM, the numerator and the denominator share no common factors. A fraction with a numerator larger than its denominator is an IMPROPER FRACTION; when the denominator is larger, it's a PROPER FRACTION.

Improper fractions can be converted into proper fractions by dividing the numerator by the denominator. The resulting whole number is placed to the left of the fraction, and the remainder becomes the new numerator; the denominator does not change. The new number is called a MIXED NUMBER because it contains a whole number and a fraction. Mixed numbers can be turned into improper fractions through the reverse process: multiply the whole number by the denominator and add the numerator to get the new numerator.

Examples

Simplify the fraction $\frac{121}{77}$.

> 121 and 77 share a common factor of 11. So, if we divide each by 11 we can simplify the fraction:
>
> $\frac{121}{77} = \frac{11}{11} \times \frac{12}{7} = \mathbf{\frac{12}{7}}$

Convert $\frac{37}{5}$ into a proper fraction.

> Start by dividing the numerator by the denominator:
>
> $37 \div 5 = 7$ with a remainder of 2
>
> Now build a mixed number with the whole number and the new numerator:
>
> $$\frac{37}{5} = 7\frac{2}{5}$$

Multiplying and Dividing Fractions

To multiply fractions, convert any mixed numbers into improper fractions and multiply the numerators together and the denominators together. Reduce to lowest terms if needed.

To divide fractions, first convert any mixed fractions into single fractions. Then, invert the second fraction so that the denominator and numerator are switched. Finally, multiply the numerators together and the denominators together.

Inverting a fraction changes multiplication to division:
$$\frac{a}{b} \div \frac{c}{d} = \frac{a}{b} \times \frac{d}{c} = \frac{ad}{bc}$$

Examples

What is the product of $\frac{1}{12}$ and $\frac{6}{8}$?

> This is a fraction multiplication problem, so simply multiply the numerators together and the denominators together and then reduce:
>
> $$\frac{1}{12} \times \frac{6}{8} = \frac{6}{96} = \frac{1}{16}$$
>
> Sometimes it's easier to reduce fractions (if you can) before multiplying:
>
> $$\frac{1}{12} \times \frac{6}{8} = \frac{1}{12} \times \frac{3}{4} = \frac{3}{48} = \frac{1}{16}$$

Find $\frac{7}{8} \div \frac{1}{4}$.

> For a fraction division problem, invert the second fraction and then multiply and reduce:
>
> $$\frac{7}{8} \div \frac{1}{4} = \frac{7}{8} \times \frac{4}{1} = \frac{28}{8} = \frac{7}{2}$$

The quotient is the result you get when you divide two numbers.

What is the quotient of $\frac{2}{5} \div 1\frac{1}{5}$?

> This is a fraction division problem, so the first step is to convert the mixed number to an improper fraction:
>
> $$1\frac{1}{5} = \frac{5 \times 1}{5} + \frac{1}{5} = \frac{6}{5}$$
>
> Now, divide the fractions. Remember to invert the second fraction, and then multiply normally:
>
> $$\frac{2}{5} \div \frac{6}{5} = \frac{2}{5} \times \frac{5}{6} = \frac{10}{30} = \frac{1}{3}$$

$\longrightarrow$
CONTINUE

A recipe calls for $\frac{1}{4}$ cup of sugar. If 8.5 batches of the recipe are needed, how many cups of sugar will be used?

This is a fraction multiplication problem: $\frac{1}{4} \times 8\frac{1}{2}$.

First, we need to convert the mixed number into a proper fraction:

$$8\frac{1}{2} = \frac{8 \times 2}{2} + \frac{1}{2} = \frac{17}{2}$$

Now, multiply the fractions across the numerators and denominators, and then reduce:

$$\frac{1}{4} \times 8\frac{1}{2} = \frac{1}{4} \times \frac{17}{2} = \frac{\mathbf{17}}{\mathbf{8}} \text{ cups of sugar}$$

Adding and Subtracting Fractions

Adding and subtracting fractions requires a COMMON DENOMINATOR. To find the common denominator, you can multiply each fraction by the number 1. With fractions, any number over itself (e.g., $\frac{5}{5}$, $\frac{12}{12}$, etc.) is equivalent to 1, so multiplying by such a fraction can change the denominator without changing the value of the fraction. Once the denominators are the same, the numerators can be added or subtracted.

To add mixed numbers, you can first add the whole numbers and then the fractions. To subtract mixed numbers, convert each number to an improper fraction, then subtract the numerators.

The phrase *simplify the expression* just means you need to perform all the operations in the expression.

Examples

Simplify the expression $\frac{2}{3} - \frac{1}{5}$.

First, multiply each fraction by a factor of 1 to get a common denominator. How do you know which factor of 1 to use? Look at the other fraction and use the number found in that denominator:

$$\frac{2}{3} - \frac{1}{5} = \frac{2}{3}\left(\frac{5}{5}\right) - \frac{1}{5}\left(\frac{3}{3}\right) = \frac{10}{15} - \frac{3}{15}$$

Once the fractions have a common denominator, simply subtract the numerators:

$$\frac{10}{15} - \frac{3}{15} = \frac{\mathbf{7}}{\mathbf{15}}$$

Find $2\frac{1}{3} - \frac{3}{2}$.

This is a fraction subtraction problem with a mixed number, so the first step is to convert the mixed number to an improper fraction:

$$2\frac{1}{3} = \frac{2 \times 3}{3} + \frac{1}{3} = \frac{7}{3}$$

Next, convert each fraction so they share a common denominator:

$$\frac{7}{3} \times \frac{2}{2} = \frac{14}{6}$$

$$\frac{3}{2} \times \frac{3}{3} = \frac{9}{6}$$

Now, subtract the fractions by subtracting the numerators:

$$\frac{14}{6} - \frac{9}{6} = \frac{\mathbf{5}}{\mathbf{6}}$$

Find the sum of $\frac{9}{16}$, $\frac{1}{2}$, and $\frac{7}{4}$.

For this fraction addition problem, we need to find a common denominator. Notice that 2 and 4 are both factors of 16, so 16 can be the common denominator:

$$\frac{1}{2} \times \frac{8}{8} = \frac{8}{16}$$

$$\frac{7}{4} \times \frac{4}{4} = \frac{28}{16}$$

$$\frac{9}{16} + \frac{8}{16} + \frac{28}{16} = \mathbf{\frac{45}{16}}$$

Sabrina has $\frac{2}{3}$ of a can of red paint. Her friend Amos has $\frac{1}{6}$ of a can. How much red paint do they have combined?

To add fractions, make sure that they have a common denominator. Since 3 is a factor of 6, 6 can be the common denominator:

$$\frac{2}{3} \times \frac{2}{2} = \frac{4}{6}$$

Now, add the numerators:

$$\frac{4}{6} + \frac{1}{6} = \mathbf{\frac{5}{6} \text{ of a can}}$$

Converting Fractions to Decimals

Calculators are not allowed on the CBEST, which can make handling fractions and decimals intimidating for many test-takers. However, there are several techniques you can use to help you convert between the two forms.

The first thing to do is simply memorize common decimals and their fractional equivalents; a list of these is given below. With these values, it's possible to convert more complicated fractions as well. For example, $\frac{2}{5}$ is just $\frac{1}{5}$ multiplied by 2, so $\frac{2}{5} = 0.2 \times 2 = 0.4$.

Table 1.3. Fraction to Decimal Conversions

FRACTION	DECIMAL
$\frac{1}{2}$	0.5
$\frac{1}{3}$	$0.\overline{33}$
$\frac{1}{4}$	0.25
$\frac{1}{5}$	0.2
$\frac{1}{6}$	$0.1\overline{66}$
$\frac{1}{7}$	$0.\overline{142857}$
$\frac{1}{8}$	0.125
$\frac{1}{9}$	$0.\overline{11}$
$\frac{1}{10}$	0.1

Knowledge of common decimal equivalents to fractions can also help you estimate. This skill can be particularly helpful on multiple-choice tests like the CBEST, where excluding incorrect answers can be just as helpful as knowing how to find the right one. For example, for a question where you must find $\frac{5}{8}$ in decimal form, you can eliminate any answers less than 0.5 because $\frac{4}{8} = 0.5$. You may also know that $\frac{6}{8}$ is the same as $\frac{3}{4}$ or 0.75, so anything above 0.75 can be eliminated as well.

Another helpful trick can be used if the denominator is easily divisible by 100: in the fraction $\frac{9}{20}$, you know 20 goes into 100 five times, so you can multiply the top and bottom by 5 to get $\frac{45}{100}$ or 0.45.

If none of these techniques work, you'll need to find the decimal by dividing the denominator by the numerator using long division.

Example

Write $\frac{8}{18}$ as a decimal.

The first step here is to simplify the fraction:

$$\frac{8}{18} = \frac{4}{9}$$

Now it's clear that the fraction is a multiple of $\frac{1}{9}$, so you can easily find the decimal using a value you already know:

$$\frac{4}{9} = \frac{1}{9} \times 4 = 0.\overline{11} \times 4 = \mathbf{0.\overline{44}}$$

Write the fraction $\frac{3}{16}$ as a decimal.

None of the tricks above will work for this fraction, so you need to do long division:

```
        0.1875
  16 | 3.0000
     - 1 6
       1 40
     - 1 28
         120
     -   112
          80
     -    80
           0
```

The decimal will go in front of the answer, so now you know that $\frac{3}{16} = \mathbf{0.1875}$.

Converting Decimals to Fractions

Converting a decimal into a fraction is more straightforward than the reverse process is. To convert a decimal, simply use the numbers that come after the decimal as the numerator in the fraction. The denominator will be a power of 10 that matches the place value for the original decimal. For example, the numerator for 0.46 would be 100 because the last number is in the tenths place; likewise, the denominator for

0.657 would be 1000 because the last number is in the thousandths place. Once this fraction has been set up, all that's left is to simplify it.

Example

Convert 0.45 into a fraction.

The last number in the decimal is in the hundredths place, so we can easily set up a fraction:

$0.45 = \frac{45}{100}$

The next step is to simply reduce the fraction down to the lowest common denominator. Here, both 45 and 100 are divisible by 5: 45 divided by 5 is 9, and 100 divided by 5 is 20. Therefore, you're left with:

$\frac{45}{100} = \frac{9}{20}$

RATIOS

A **RATIO** tells you how many of one thing exists in relation to the number of another thing. Unlike fractions, ratios do not give a part relative to a whole; instead, it's comparing two values. For example, if you have 3 apples and 4 oranges, the ratio of apples to oranges is 3 to 4. Ratios can be written using words (3 to 4), fractions $\left(\frac{3}{4}\right)$, or colons (3:4).

In order to work with ratios, it's helpful to rewrite them as a fraction expressing a part to a whole. For example, in the example above you have 7 total pieces of fruit, so the fraction of your fruit that are apples is $\frac{3}{7}$, and oranges make up $\frac{4}{7}$ of your fruit collection.

One last important thing to consider when working with ratios is the units of the values being compared. On the CBEST, you may be asked to rewrite a ratio using the same units on both sides. For example, you might have to rewrite the ratio 3 minutes to 7 seconds as 180 seconds to 7 seconds.

Examples

There are 90 voters in a room, and each is either a Democrat or a Republican. The ratio of Democrats to Republicans is 5:4. How many Republicans are there?

We know that there are 5 Democrats for every 4 Republicans in the room, which means for every 9 people, 4 are Republicans.

$5 + 4 = 9$

Fraction of Democrats: $\frac{5}{9}$

Fraction of Republicans: $\frac{4}{9}$

If $\frac{4}{9}$ of the 90 voters are Republicans, then:

$\frac{4}{9} \times 90 =$ **40 voters are Republicans**

CONTINUE

The ratio of students to teachers in a school is 15:1. If there are 38 teachers, how many students attend the school?

To solve this ratio problem, we can simply multiply both sides of the ratio by the desired value to find the number of students that correspond to having 38 teachers:

$$\frac{15 \text{ students}}{1 \text{ teacher}} \times \frac{38}{38} = \frac{570 \text{ students}}{15 \text{ teachers}}$$

The school has **570 students**.

PROPORTIONS

A proportion is an equation which states that two ratios are equal. Proportions are usually written as two fractions joined by an equal sign $\left(\frac{a}{b} = \frac{c}{d}\right)$, but they can also be written using colons (a : b :: c : d). Note that in a proportion, the units must be the same in both numerators and in both denominators.

Often you will be given 3 of the values in a proportion and asked to find the 4th. In these types of problems, you can solve for the missing variable by cross-multiplying—multiply the numerator of each fraction by the denominator of the other to get an equation with no fractions as shown below. You can then solve the equation using basic algebra.

$$\frac{a}{b} = \frac{c}{d} \rightarrow ad = bc$$

Examples

A train traveling 120 miles takes 3 hours to get to its destination. How long will it take for the train to travel 180 miles?

Start by setting up the proportion:

$$\frac{120 \text{ miles}}{3 \text{ hours}} = \frac{180 \text{ miles}}{x \text{ hours}}$$

Note that it doesn't matter which value is placed in the numerator or denominator, as long as it is the same on both sides. Now, solve for the missing quantity through cross–multiplication:

120 miles × x hours = 3 hours × 180 miles

Now solve the equation:

$$x \text{ hours} = \frac{(3 \text{ hours}) \times (180 \text{ miles})}{120 \text{ miles}}$$

$x = 4.5$ hours

One acre of wheat requires 500 gallons of water. How many acres can be watered with 2600 gallons?

Set up the equation:

$$\frac{1 \text{ acre}}{500 \text{ gal.}} = \frac{x \text{ acres}}{2600 \text{ gal.}}$$

Then solve for x:

$$x \text{ acres} = \frac{1 \text{ acre} \times 2600 \text{ gal.}}{500 \text{ gal.}}$$

$x = \frac{26}{5}$ or **5.2 acres**

For more on solving basic equation, see *Algebraic Expressions and Equations*.

If 35 : 5 :: 49 : x, find x.

This problem presents two equivalent ratios that can be set up in a fraction equation:

$$\frac{35}{5} = \frac{49}{x}$$

You can then cross-multiply to solve for x:

$$35x = 49 \times 5$$

$$x = \mathbf{7}$$

PERCENTAGES

A **PERCENT** is the ratio of a part to the whole. Questions may give the part and the whole and ask for the percent, or give the percent and the whole and ask for the part, or give the part and the percent and ask for the value of the whole. The equation for percentages can be rearranged to solve for any of these:

$$percent = \frac{part}{whole}$$

$$part = whole \times percent$$

$$whole = \frac{part}{percent}$$

In the equations above, the percent should always be expressed as a decimal. In order to convert a decimal into a percentage value, simply multiply it by 100. So, If you've read 5 pages (the part) of a 10 page article (the whole), you've read $\frac{5}{10}$ = .50 or 50%. (The percent sign (%) is used once the decimal has been multiplied by 100.)

Note that when solving these problems, the units for the part and the whole should be the same. If you're reading a book, saying you've read 5 pages out of 15 chapters doesn't make any sense.

The word *of* usually indicates the whole in a problem. For example, the problem might say *Ella ate 2 slices of the pizza*, which means the pizza is the whole.

Examples

45 is 15% of what number?

Set up the appropriate equation and solve. Don't forget to change 15% to a decimal value:

$$whole = \frac{part}{percent} = \frac{45}{0.15} = \mathbf{300}$$

Jim spent 30% of his paycheck at the fair. He spent $15 for a hat, $30 for a shirt, and $20 playing games. How much was his check? (Round to nearest dollar.)

Set up the appropriate equation and solve:

$$whole = \frac{part}{percent} = \frac{15 + 30 + 20}{.30} = \mathbf{\$217.00}$$

What percent of 65 is 39?

Set up the equation and solve:

$$percent = \frac{part}{whole} = \frac{39}{65} = \mathbf{0.6 \text{ or } 60\%}$$

Greta and Max sell cable subscriptions. In a given month, Greta sells 45 subscriptions and Max sells 51. If 240 total subscriptions were sold in that month, what percent were not sold by Greta or Max?

You can use the information in the question to figure out what percentage of subscriptions were sold by Max and Greta:

$percent = \dfrac{part}{whole} = 51 + \dfrac{45}{240} = 0.4$ or 40%

However, the question asks how many subscriptions weren't sold by Max or Greta. If they sold 40%, then the other salespeople sold 100% − 40% = **60%**.

Grant needs to score 75% on an exam. If the exam has 45 questions, at least how many does he need to answer correctly?

Set up the equation and solve. Remember to convert 75% to a decimal value:

$part = whole \times percent = 45 \times 0.75 = 33.75$, so he needs to answer at least **34 questions correctly**.

Percent Change

PERCENT CHANGE problems will ask you to calculate how much a given quantity changed. The problems are solving in a similar way to regular percent problems, except that instead of using the "part" you'll use the "amount of change." Note that the sign of the "amount of change" is important: if the original amount has increased the change will be positive, and if it has decreases the change will be negative. Again, in the equations below the percent is a decimal value; you need to multiply by 100 to get the actual percentage.

$$percent\ change = \dfrac{amount\ of\ change}{original\ amount}$$

$$amount\ of\ change = original\ amount \times percent\ change$$

$$original\ amount = \dfrac{amount\ of\ change}{percent\ change}$$

Words that indicate a percent change problem:
- discount
- markup
- sale
- increase
- decrease

The same steps shown here can be used to find percent change for problems that don't involve money as well.

Examples

A computer software retailer marks up its games by 40% above the wholesale price when it sells them to customer. Find the price of a game for a customer if the game cost the retailer $25.

Set up the appropriate equation and solve:

$amount\ of\ change = original\ amount \times percent\ change = 25 \times 0.4 = 10$

If the amount of change is 10, that means the store adds a markup of $10, so the game costs:

$25 + $10 = **$35**

A golf shop pays its wholesaler $40 for a certain club, and then sells it to a golfer for $75. What is the markup rate?

First, calculate the amount of change:

$75 - 40 = 35$

Now you can set up the equation and solve. (Note that *markup rate* is another way of saying *percent change*):

$percent\ change = \dfrac{amount\ of\ change}{original\ amount} = \dfrac{35}{40} = 0.875 = \textbf{87.5\%}$

A shoe store charges a 40% markup on the shoes it sells. How much did the store pay for a pair of shoes purchased by a customer for $63?

You're solving for the original price, but it's going to be tricky because you don't know the amount of change; you only know the new price. To solve, you need to create an expression for the amount of change:

If *original amount* $= x$

Then *amount of change* $= 63 - x$

Now you can plug these values into your equation:

original amount = *amount of change/percent change*

$x = \dfrac{63 - x}{0.4}$

The last step is to solve for x:

$0.4x = 63 - x$

$1.4x = 63$

$x = 45$

The store paid **$45** for the shoes.

An item originally priced at $55 is marked 25% off. What is the sale price?

You've been asked to find the sale price, which means you need to solve for the amount of change first:

amount of change = original amount x percent change =
$55 \times 0.25 = 13.75$

Using this amount, you can find the new price. Because it's on sale, we know the item will cost less than the original price:

$55 - 13.75 = 41.25$

The sale price is **$41.25**.

James wants to put in an 18 foot by 51 foot garden in his backyard. If he does, it will reduce the size of this yard by 24%. What will be the area of the remaining yard?

This problem is tricky because you need to figure out what each number in the problem stands for. 24% is obviously the percent change, but what about the measurements in feet? If you multiply these values you get the area of the garden (for more on area see *Area and Perimeter*):

CONTINUE

18 ft. × 51 ft. = 918 ft.²

This 918 ft.² is the amount of change—it's how much smaller the lawn is. Now we can set up an equation:

$original\ amount = \frac{amount\ of\ change}{percent\ change} = \frac{918}{24} = 3825$

If the original lawn was 3825 ft.² and the garden is 918 ft.², then the remaining area is

3825 − 918 = 2907

The remaining lawn covers **2907 ft.²**

COMPARISON OF RATIONAL NUMBERS

Number comparison problems present numbers in different formats and ask which is larger or smaller, or whether the numbers are equivalent. The important step in solving these problems is to convert the numbers to the same format so that it is easier to see how they compare. If numbers are given in the same format, or after they have been converted, determine which number is smaller or if the numbers are equal. Remember that for negative numbers, higher numbers are actually smaller.

The strategies for comparing numbers can also be used to put numbers in order from least to greatest (or vice versa).

Examples

Is $4\frac{3}{4}$ greater than, equal to, or less than $\frac{18}{4}$?

These numbers are in different formats—one is a mixed fraction and the other is just a fraction. So, the first step is to convert the mixed fraction to a fraction:

$4\frac{3}{4} = 4 \times \frac{4}{4} + \frac{3}{4} = \frac{19}{4}$

Once the mixed number is converted, it is easier to see that $\frac{19}{4}$ **is greater than** $\frac{18}{4}$.

Which of the following numbers has the greatest value: 104.56, 104.5, or 104.6?

These numbers are already in the same format, so the decimal values just need to be compared. Remember that zeros can be added after the decimal without changing the value, so the three numbers can be rewritten as:

104.56

104.50

104.60

From this list, it is clearer to see that 104.60 is the greatest because 0.60 is larger than 0.50 and 0.56.

Is 65% greater than, less than, or equal to $\frac{13}{20}$?

The first step is to convert the numbers into the same format. 65% is the same as $\frac{65}{100}$.

Next, the fractions need to be converted to have the same denominator. It is difficult to compare fractions with different denominators. Using a factor of $\frac{5}{5}$ on the second fraction will give common denominators:

$\frac{13}{20} \times \frac{5}{5} = \frac{65}{100}$.

Now, it is easy to see that **the numbers are equivalent**.

GEOMETRY

Geometry is the study of shapes. On the CBEST, you'll need to be able to find the perimeter and area of two-dimensional shapes and the volume of three-dimensional shapes. These problems will require you to use a variety of units, so make sure you're comfortable with all the information in tables 1.1 and 1.2.

PROPERTY OF SHAPES: AREA AND PERIMETER

AREA and PERIMETER problems will require you to use the equations shown in the table below to find either the area inside a shape or the distance around it (the perimeter). These equations will not be given on the test, so you need to have them memorized on test day.

Table 3.1. Equations

SHAPE	AREA	PERIMETER
circle	$A = \pi r^2$	$C = 2\pi r = \pi d$
triangle	$A = \frac{b \times h}{2}$	$P = s^1 + s^2 + s^3$
square	$A = s^2$	$P = 4s$
rectangle	$A = l \times w$	$P = 2l + 2$

These equations aren't given to you on test day—you need to have them memorized.

Examples

A farmer has purchased 100 m of fencing to put around his rectangular garden. If one side of the garden is 20 m long and the other is 28 m, how much fencing will the farmer have left over?

The perimeter of a rectangle is equal to twice its length plus twice its width:

$P = 2(20) + 2(28) + 96$ m

The farmer has 100 m of fencing, so he'll have 100 − 96 = **4 m** left.

Taylor is going to paint a square wall that is 3.5 m tall. How much paint will he need?

Each side of the square wall is 3.5 m:

$A = 3.5^2 =$ **12.25 m**

ALGEBRA

The topics covered in algebra will be the most heavily tested on the CBEST, and a basic understanding of algebra is also necessary to complete many of the questions on other topics. The topics covered in this chapter include expressions, linear and quadratic equations, and word problems.

ALGEBRAIC EXPRESSIONS

Algebraic expressions and equations include a VARIABLE, which is a letter standing in for a number. These expressions and equations are made up of TERMS, which are groups of numbers and variables (e.g., $2xy$). An EXPRESSION is simply a set of terms (e.g., $3x + 2xy$), while an EQUATION includes an equal sign (e.g., $3x + 2xy = 17$). When simplifying expressions or solving algebraic equations, you'll need to use many different mathematical properties and operations, including addition/subtraction, multiplication/division, exponents, roots, distribution, and the order of operations.

Evaluating Algebraic Expressions

To evaluate an algebraic expression, simply plug the given value(s) in for the appropriate variable(s) in the expression.

Example

Evaluate $2x + 6y - 3z$ if , $x = 2$, and $z = -3$.

Plug in each number for the correct variable and simplify:

$2x + 6y - 3z = 2(2) + 6(4) - 3(-3) = 4 + 24 + 9 = \mathbf{37}$

Adding and Subtracting Terms

Only LIKE TERMS, which have the exact same variable(s), can be added or subtracted. CONSTANTS are numbers without variables attached, and those can be added and subtracted together as well. When simplifying an expression, like terms should be added or subtracted so that no individual group of variables occurs in more than one term. For example, the expression $5x + 6xy$ is in its simplest form, while $5x + 6xy - 11xy$ is not because the term xy appears more than once.

Example

Simplify the expression $5xy + 7y + 2yz + 11xy - 5yz$.

Start by grouping together like terms:

$(5xy + 11xy) + (2yz - 5yz) + 7y$

Now you can add together each set of like terms:

$16xy + 7y - 3yz$

Multiplying and Dividing Terms

To multiply a single term by another, simply multiply the coefficients and then multiply the variables. Remember that when multiplying variables with exponents, those exponents are added together. For example, $(x^5y)(x^3y^4) = x^8y^5$.

When multiplying a term by a set of terms inside parentheses, you need to DISTRIBUTE to each term inside the parentheses as shown below:

$$a(b+c) = ab + ac$$

Figure 2.1. Distribution

When variables occur in both the numerator and denominator of a fraction, they cancel each other out. So, a fraction with variables in its simplest form will not have the same variable on the top and bottom.

Examples

Simplify the expression $(3x^4y^2z)(2y^4z^5)$.

Multiply the coefficients and variables together:

$3 \times 2 = 6$

$y^2 \times y^4 = y^6$

$z \times z^5 = z^6$

Now put all the terms back together:

$6x^4y^6z^6$

Simplify the expression: $(2y^2)(y^3 + 2xy^2z + 4z)$

Multiply each term inside the parentheses by the term $2y^2$:

$(2y^2)(y^3 + 2xy^2z + 4z) =$

$(2y^2 \times y^3) + (2y^2 \times 2xy^2 z) \times (2y^2 \times 4z) =$

$2y^5 + 4xy^4z + 8y^2z$

Simplify the expression: $(5x + 2)(3x + 3)$

Use the acronym FOIL—first, outer, inner, last—to multiply the terms:

First: $5x \times 3x = 15x^2$

Outer: $5x \times 3 = 15x$

Inner: $2 \times 3x = 6x$

Last: $2 \times 3 = 6$

Now combine like terms:

$15x^2 + 21x + 6$

Simplify the expression: $\frac{2x^4y^3z}{8x^2z^2}$

Simplify by looking at each variable and crossing those that appear in the numerator and denominator:

$$\frac{2}{8} = \frac{1}{4}$$

$$\frac{x^4}{x^2} = \frac{x^2}{1}$$

$$\frac{z}{z^2} = \frac{1}{z}$$

$$\frac{2x^4y^3z}{8x^2z^2} = \frac{x^2y^3}{4z} \text{ f}$$

When multiplying terms, add the exponents. When dividing, subtract the exponents.

Factoring Expressions

Factoring is splitting one expression into the multiplication of two expressions. It requires finding the highest common factor and dividing terms by that number. For example, in the expression $15x + 10$, the highest common factor is 5 because both terms are divisible by 5: $\frac{15x}{5} = 3x$ and $\frac{10}{5} = 2$. When you factor the expression you get $5(3x + 2)$.

Sometimes it is not so easy to find the highest common factor. In these cases, consider whether the expression fits a polynomial identity. A polynomial is an expression with more than one term. If you can recognize the common polynomials listed below, you can easily factor the expression.

$a^2 - b^2 = (a + b)(a - b)$

$a^2 + 2ab + b^2 = (a + b)(a + b) = (a + b)^2$

$a^2 - 2ab + b^2 = (a - b)(a - b) = (a - b)^2$

$a^3 + b^3 = (a + b)(a^2 - ab - b^2)$

$a^3 - b^3 = (a - b)(a^2 + ab + b^2)$

CONTINUE

Examples

Factor the expression $27x^2 - 9x$

> First, find the highest common factor. Both terms are divisible by 9:
>
> $\frac{(27x^2)}{9} = 3x^2$ and $\frac{9x}{9} = x$
>
> Now our expression is $9(3x^2 - x)$ – but wait, we are not done! Both terms can be divided by x:
>
> $\frac{3x^2}{x} = 3x$ and $\frac{x}{x} = 1$.
>
> The final factored expression is $\mathbf{9x(3x - 1)}$.

Factor the expression $25x^2 - 16$

> Since there is no obvious factor by which we can divide terms, we should consider whether this expression fits one of our polynomial identities.
>
> This expression is a difference of squares $a^2 - b^2$, where $a^2 = 25x^2$ and $b^2 = 16$.
>
> Recall that $a^2 - b^2 = (a + b)(a - b)$. Now solve for a and b:
>
> $a = \sqrt{25x^2} = 5x$
>
> $b = \sqrt{16} = 4$
>
> $(a + b)(a - b) = (5x + 4)(5x - 4)$
>
> You can check your work by using the FOIL acronym to expand your answer back to the original expression:
>
> First: $5x \times 5x = 25x^2$
>
> Outer: $5x \times -4 = -20x$
>
> Inner: $4 \times 5x = 20x$
>
> Last: $4 \times -4 = -16$
>
> $\mathbf{25x^2 - 20x + 20x - 16 = 25x^2 - 16}$

Factor the expression $100x^2 + 60x + 9$

> This is another polynomial identity, $a^2 + 2ab + b^2$. (The more practice you have with these problems, the faster you will become at identifying the polynomial identities.)
>
> $a^2 = 100x^2$, $2ab = 60x$, and $b^2 = 9$
>
> Recall that $a^2 + 2ab + b^2 = (a + b)^2$. Now solve for a and b:
>
> $a = \sqrt{\mathbf{100x^2}} = \mathbf{10x}$
>
> $b = \sqrt{\mathbf{9}} = \mathbf{3}$
>
> (Double check your work by confirming that $2ab = 2 \times 10x \times 3 = 60x$)
>
> $(a + b)^2 = \mathbf{(10x + 3)^2}$

LINEAR EQUATIONS

An **EQUATION** is a statement saying that two expressions are equal to each other. They always include an equal sign (e.g., $3x + 2xy = 17$). A **LINEAR EQUATION** has only two variables; on a graph, linear equations form a straight line.

Solving Linear Equations

To solve an equation, you need to manipulate the terms on each side to isolate the variable, meaning if you want to find x, you have to get the x alone on one side of the equal sign. To do this, you'll need to use many of the tools discussed above: you might need to distribute, divide, add or subtract like terms, or find common denominators.

Think of each side of the equation as the two sides of a see-saw. As long as the two people on each end weigh the same amount (no matter what it is) the see-saw will be balanced: if you have a 120 lb. person on each end, the see-saw is balanced. Giving each of them a 10 lb. rock to hold changes the weight on each end, but the see-saw itself stays balanced. Equations work the same way: you can add, subtract, multiply, or divide whatever you want as long as you do the same thing to both sides.

Most equations you'll see on the CBEST can be solved using the same basic steps:

1. Distribute to get rid of parentheses.
2. Use the least common denominator to get rid of fractions.
3. Add/subtract like terms on either side.
4. Add/subtract so that constants appear on only one side of the equation.
5. Multiply/divide to isolate the variable.

Examples

Solve for x: $25x + 12 = 62$

> This equation has no parentheses, fractions, or like terms on the same side, so you can start by subtracting 12 from both sides of the equation:
>
> $25x + 12 = 62$
>
> $(25x + 12) - 12 = 62 - 12$
>
> $25x = 50$
>
> Now, divide by 25 to isolate the variable:
>
> $\frac{25x}{25} = \frac{50}{25}$
>
> $\boldsymbol{x = 2}$

→

CONTINUE

Solve the following equation for x: $2x\ 4(2x + 3) = 24$

Start by distributing to get rid of the parentheses (don't forget to distribute the negative):

$2x - 4(2x + 3) = 24 \rightarrow$

$2x - 8x - 12 = 24$

There are no fractions, so now you can join like terms:

$2x - 8x - 12 = 24 \rightarrow$

$-6x - 12 = 24$

Now add 12 to both sides and divide by -6.

$-6x - 12 = 24$

$(-6x - 12) + 12 = 24 + 12 \rightarrow$

$-6x = 36 \rightarrow$

$\frac{-6x}{-6} = \frac{36}{-6}$

$x = -6$

Solve the following equation for x: $\frac{x}{3} + \frac{1}{2} = \frac{x}{6} - \frac{5}{12}$

Start by multiplying by the least common denominator to get rid of the fractions:

$\frac{x}{3} + \frac{1}{2} = \frac{x}{6} - \frac{5}{12} \rightarrow$

$12\left(\frac{x}{3} + \frac{1}{2}\right) = 12\left(\frac{x}{6} - \frac{5}{12}\right) \rightarrow$

$4x + 6 = 2x - 5$

Now you can isolate x:

$(4x + 6) - 6 = (2x - 5) - 6 \rightarrow$

$4x = 2x - 11 \rightarrow$

$(4x) - 2x = (2x - 11) - 2x \rightarrow$

$2x = -11$

$x = -\frac{11}{2}$

Find the value of x: $2(x + y) - 7x = 14x + 3$

This equation looks more difficult because it has 2 variables, but you can use the same steps to solve for x. First, distribute to get rid of the parentheses and combine like terms:

$2(x + y) - 7x = 14x + 3 \rightarrow$

$2x + 2y - 7x = 14x + 3 \rightarrow$

$-5x + 2y = 14x + 3$

Now you can move the x terms to one side and everything else to the other, and then divide to isolate x:

$-5x + 2y = 14x + 3 \rightarrow$

$-19x = -2y + 3 \rightarrow$

$x = \frac{2y - 3}{19}$

Building Equations

Word problems describe a situation or a problem without explicitly providing an equation to solve. It is up to you to build an algebraic equation to solve the problem. You must translate the words into mathematical operations. Represent the quantity you do not know by a variable. If there is more than one unknown, you will likely have to write more than one equation, then solve the system of equations by substituting expressions. Make sure you keep your variables straight!

Examples

David, Jesse and Mark shoveled snow during their snow day and made a total of $100. They agreed to split it based on how much each person worked. David will take $10 more than Jesse, who will take $15 more than Mark. How much money will David get?

Start by building an equation. David's amount will be d, Jesse's amount will be j, and Mark's amount will be m. All three must add up to $100:

$d + j + m = 100$

It may seem like there are three unknowns in this situation, but we can express j and m in terms of d:

Jesse gets $10 less than David, so $j = d - 10$. Mark gets $15 less than Jesse, so $m = j - 15$.

Substituting the previous expression for j to solve for m in terms of d:

$m = (d - 10) - 15 = d - 25$

Now back to our original equation, substituting for j and m:

$d + (d - 10) + (d - 25) = 100$

$3d - 35 = 100$

$3d = 135$

$d = \mathbf{45}$

David will get $45.

The sum of three consecutive numbers is 54. What is the middle number?

Start by building an equation. One of the numbers in question will be x. The three numbers are consecutive, so if x is the smallest number then the other two numbers must be $(x + 1)$ and $(x - 1)$. We know that the sum of the three numbers is 54:

$x + (x + 1) + (x + 2) = 54$

Now solve for the equation to find x:

$3x + 3 = 54$

$3x = 51$

$x = 17$

The question asks about the middle number $(x + 1)$, so the answer is 18.

Notice that we could have picked any number to be x. If we picked the middle number as x, our equation would be

$(x - 1) + x + (x + 1) = 54$. **Solve for x to get 18.**

There are 42 people on the varsity football team. This is 8 more than half the number of people on the swim team. There are 6 fewer boys on the swim team than girls. How many girls are on the swim team?

This word problem might seem complicated at first, but as long as we keep our variables straight and translate the words into mathematical operations we can easily build an equation. The quantity we want to solve is the number of girls on the swim team, so this will be x.

The number of boys on the swim team will be y. There are 6 fewer boys than girls so $y = x - 6$.

The total number of boys and girls on the swim team is $x + y$.

42 is 8 more than half this number, so $42 = 8 + (x + y) \div 2$

Now substitute for y to solve for x:

$42 = 8 + (x + x - 7) \div 2$

$34 = (2x - 6) \div 2$

$68 = 2x - 6$

$74 = 2x$

$x = \mathbf{37}$

There are 37 girls on the swim team.

LINEAR INEQUALITIES

INEQUALITIES look like equations, except that instead of having an equal sign, they have one of the following symbols:

\> Greater than: The expression left of the symbol is larger than the expression on the right.

\< Less than: The expression left of the symbol is smaller than the expression on the right.

≥ Greater than or equal to: The expression left of the symbol is larger than or equal to the expression on the right.

≤ Less than or equal to: The expression left of the symbol is less than or equal to the expression on the right.

Inequalities are solved like linear and other algebraic equations. The only difference is that the symbol must be reversed when both sides of the equation are multiplied by a negative number.

Example

Solve for x: $-7x + 2 < 6 - 5x$

> Collect like terms on each side as you would for a regular equation:
>
> $-7x + 2 < 6 - 5x \rightarrow$
>
> $-2x < 4$
>
> The direction of the sign switches when you divide by a negative number:
>
> $-2x < 4 \rightarrow$
>
> $\mathbf{x > -2}$

See *Solving Linear Equations* for step-by-step instructions on solving basic equations.

SOLVING WORD PROBLEMS

Any of the math concepts discussed here can be turned into a word problem, and you'll likely see word problems in various forms throughout the test. (In fact, you may have noticed that several examples in the ratio and proportion sections were word problems.)

The most important step in solving any word problem is to read the entire problem before beginning to solve it: one of the most commonly made mistakes on word problems is providing an answer to a question that wasn't asked. Also, remember that not all of the information given in a problem is always needed to solve it.

When working multiple-choice word problems like those on the CBEST, it's important to check your answer. Many of the incorrect choices will be answers that test-takers arrive at by making common mistakes. So even if an answer you calculated is a given as an answer choice, that doesn't necessarily mean you've worked the problem correctly—you have to check your own work to make sure.

General Steps for Word Problem Solving

Step 1: Read the entire problem and determine what the question is asking for.

Step 2: List all of the given data and define the variables.

Step 3: Determine the formula(s) needed or set up equations from the information in the problem.

Step 4: Solve.

Step 5: Check your answer. (Is the amount too large or small? Are the answers in the correct unit of measure?)

Basic Word Problems

A word problem in algebra is just an equation or a set of equations described using words. Your task when solving these problems is to turn the *story* of the problem into mathematical equations.

KEY WORDS

Word Problems generally contain key words that can help you determine what math processes may be required in order to solve them.

- Addition: added, combined, increased by, in all, total, perimeter, sum, more than
- Subtraction: how much more, less than, fewer than, exceeds, difference, decreased
- Multiplication: of, times, area, product
- Division: distribute, share, average, per, out of, percent, quotient
- Equals: is, was, are, amounts to, were

CONTINUE

Examples

A store owner bought a case of 48 backpacks for $476.00. He sold 17 of the backpacks in his store for $18 each, and the rest were sold to a school for $15 each. What was the salesman's profit?

Start by listing all the data and defining the variable:

total number of backpacks = 48

cost of backpacks = $476.00

backpacks sold in store at price of $18 = 17

backpacks sold to school at a price of $15 = 75 − 17 = 58

total profit = x

Now set up an equation:

total profit = income − cost

The store owner made a profit of **$700**.

Thirty students in Mr. Joyce's room are working on projects over 2 days. The first day, he gave them 3/5 hour to work. On the second day, he gave them half as much time as the first day. How much time did each student have to work on the project?

Start by listing all the data and defining your variables. Note that the number of students, while given in the problem, is not needed to find the answer:

time on 1st day = $\frac{3}{5}$ hr. = 36 min.

time on 2nd day = $\frac{1}{2}$(36) = 18 min.

total time = x

Now set up the equation and solve:

total time = time on 1st day + time on 2nd day

$x = 36 + 18 = 54$

The students had **54 minutes** to work on the projects.

Converting units can often help you avoid operations with fractions when dealing with time.

Distance Word Problems

Distance word problems involve something traveling at a constant or average speed. Whenever you read a problem that involves *how fast, how far,* or *for how long*, you should think of the distance equation, , where *d* stands for distance, *r* for rate (speed), and *t* for time.

These problems can be solved by setting up a grid with *d*, *r*, and *t* along the top and each moving object on the left. When setting up the grid, make sure the units are consistent. For example, if the distance is in meters and the time is in seconds, the rate should be meters per second.

Examples

Will drove from his home to the airport at an average speed of 30 mph. He then boarded a helicopter and flew to the hospital with an average speed of 60 mph. The entire distance was 150 miles, and the trip took 3 hours. Find the distance from the airport to the hospital.

The first step is to set up a table and fill in a value for each variable:

Table 2.1. Drive Time

	d	r	t
driving	d	30	t
flying	$150 - d$	60	$3 - t$

You can now set up equations for driving and flying. The first row gives the equation $d = 30t$, and the second row gives the equation $150 - d = 60(3 - t))$.

Next, you can solve this system of equations. Start by substituting for d in the second equation:

$d = 30t$

$150 - d = 60(30 - t)) \rightarrow 150 - 30t = 60(30 - t)$

Now solve for t:

$150 - 30t = 180 - 60t$

$-30 = -30t$

$1 = t$

Although you've solved for t, you're not done yet. Notice that the problem asks for distance. So, you need to solve for d: what the problem asked for. It does not ask for time, but the time is needed to solve the problem.

Driving: $30t = 30$ miles

Flying: $150 - d = 120$ miles

The distance from the airport to the hospital is **120 miles**.

Two cyclists start at the same time from opposite ends of a course that is 45 miles long. One cyclist is riding at 14 mph and the second cyclist is riding at 16 mph. How long after they begin will they meet?

First, set up the table. The variable for time will be the same for each, because they will have been on the road for the same amount of time when they meet:

Table 2.2. Cyclist Times

	d	r	t
Cyclist #1	d	14	t
Cyclist #2	$45 - d$	16	t

Nest set up two equations:

Cyclist #1: $d = 14t$

Cyclist #2: $45 - d = 16t$

Now substitute and solve:

$d = 14t$

$45 - d = 16t \rightarrow 45 - 14t = 16t$

$45 = 30t$

$t = 1.5$

They will meet **1.5 hr.** after they begin.

Work Problems

WORK PROBLEMS involve situations where several people or machines are doing work at different rates. Your task is usually to figure out how long it will take these people or machines to complete a task while working together. The trick to doing work problems is to figure out how much of the project each person or machine completes in the same unit of time. For example, you might calculate how much of a wall a person can paint in 1 hour, or how many boxes an assembly line can pack in 1 minute.

Once you know that, you can set up an equation to solve for the total time. This equation usually has a form similar to the equation for distance, but here *work = rate × time*.

The CBEST will give you most formulas you need to work problems, but they won't give you the formulas for percent change or work problems.

See *Adding and Subtracting Fractions* for step-by-step instruction on operations with fractions.

Examples

Bridget can clean an entire house in 12 hours while her brother Tom takes 8 hours. How long would it take for Bridget and Tom to clean 2 houses together?

> Start by figuring out how much of a house each sibling can clean on his or her own. Bridget can clean the house in 12 hours, so she can clean $\frac{1}{12}$ of the house in an hour. Using the same logic, Tom can clean $\frac{1}{8}$ of a house in an hour.
>
> By adding these values together, you get the fraction of the house they can paint together in an hour:
>
> $\frac{1}{12} + \frac{1}{8} = \frac{5}{24}$
>
> They can do $\frac{5}{24}$ of the job per hour.
>
> Now set up variables and an equation to solve:
>
> t = time spent cleaning (in hours)
>
> h = number of houses cleaned = 2
>
> *work = rate × time*
>
> $h = \frac{5}{24}t \rightarrow$
>
> $2 = \frac{5}{24}t \rightarrow$
>
> $t = \frac{48}{5} = 9\frac{3}{5}$ hours

Farmer Dan needs to water his cornfield. One hose can water a field 1.25 times faster than a second hose. When both hoses are opened, they water the field in 5 hours. How long would it take to water the field if only the second hose is used?

> In this problem you don't know the exact time, but you can still find the hourly rate as a variable:
>
> The second hose completes the job in f hours, so it waters $\frac{1}{f}$ field per hour. The faster hose waters the field in 1.25f, so it waters the field in $\frac{1}{1.25f}$ hours. Together, they take 5 hours to water the field, so they water $\frac{1}{5}$ of the field per hour.

Now you can set up the equations and solve:

$$\frac{1}{f} + \frac{1}{1.25f} = \frac{1}{5} \rightarrow$$

$$1.25f\left(\frac{1}{f} + \frac{1}{1.25f}\right) = 1.25f\left(\frac{1}{5}\right) \rightarrow$$

$$1.25 + 1 = 0.25f$$

$$2.25 = 0.25f$$

$$f = 9$$

The slow hose takes 9 hours to water the cornfield. The fast hose takes 1.25(9) = **11.25 hours**.

Alex takes 2 hours to shine 500 silver spoons, and Julian takes 3 hours to shine 450 silver spoons. How long will they take, working together, to shine 1000 silver spoons?

Calculate how many dishes each man can wash per hour:

Alex: $\dfrac{500 \text{ spoons}}{2 \text{ hours}} = \dfrac{250 \text{ spoons}}{\text{hour}}$

Julian: $\dfrac{450 \text{ spoons}}{3 \text{ hours}} = \dfrac{150 \text{ spoons}}{\text{hour}}$

Together: $\dfrac{(250 + 150) \text{ spoons}}{\text{hour}} = \dfrac{400 \text{ spoons}}{\text{hour}}$

Now set up an equation to find the time it takes to shine 1000 spoons:

total time $= \dfrac{1 \text{ hour}}{400 \text{ spoons}} \times 1000 \text{ spoons} = \dfrac{1000}{400} \text{ hours} = $ **2.5 hours**

STATISTICS AND PROBABILITY

DESCRIBING SETS OF DATA

STATISTICS is the study of sets of data. The goal of statistics is to take a group of values—numerical answers from a survey, for example—and look for patterns in how that data is distributed.

When looking at a set of data, it's often helpful to look at the **MEASURES OF CENTRAL TENDENCY**, which are a group of values that describe the central or typical data point from the set. The CBEST covers 3 measures of central tendency: mean, median, and mode.

MEAN is the mathematical term for average. To find the mean, total all the terms and divide by the number of terms. The **MEDIAN** is the middle number of a given set. To find the median, put the terms in numerical order; the middle number will be the median. In the case of a set of even numbers, the middle two numbers are averaged to find median. **MODE** is the number which occurs most frequently within a given set. If two different numbers both appear with the highest frequency, they are both the mode.

When examining a data set, it's also possible to look at **MEASURES OF VARIABILITY**, which describe how the data is dispersed around the central data point. The CBEST covers two measure of variability: **RANGE** and **STANDARD DEVIATION**. Range is simply the difference between the largest and smallest values in the set. Standard deviation is a measure of how dispersed the data is; in other words, it describes how far from the mean the data is.

Examples

Find the mean of 24, 27, and 18.

Add the terms then divide by the number of terms:

$$mean = \frac{24 + 27 + 18}{3} = \textbf{23}$$

The mean of three numbers is 45. If two of the numbers are 38 and 43, what is the third number?

Set up the equation for mean with x representing the third number, then solve:

$mean = \frac{38 + 43 + x}{3} = 45$

$38 + 43 + x = 135$

$x = \mathbf{54}$

What is the median of 24, 27, and 18?

Place the terms in order, then pick the middle term:

18, 24, 27

The median is **24**.

What is the median of 24, 27, 18, and 19?

Place the terms in order. Because there are an even number of terms, the median will be the average of the middle 2 terms:

18, 19, 24, 27

$median = \frac{19 + 24}{2} = \mathbf{21.5}$

What is the mode of 2, 5, 4, 4, 3, 2, 8, 9, 2, 7, 2, and 2?

The mode is 2 because it appears the most within the set.

What is the standard deviation of 62, 63, 61, and 66?

To find the standard deviation, first find the mean:

$mean = \frac{(62 + 63 + 61 + 66)}{4} = 63$

Next, find the difference between each term and the mean, and square that number:

$63 - 62 = 1 \rightarrow 1^2 = 1$

$63 - 63 = 0 \rightarrow 0^2 = 0$

$63 - 61 = 2 \rightarrow 2^2 = 4$

$63 - 66 = -3 \rightarrow (-3)^2 = 9$

Now, find the mean of the squares:

$mean = \frac{(1 + 0 + 4 + 9)}{4} = 3.5$

Finally, find the square root of the mean:

$\sqrt{3.5} = 1.87$

The standard deviation is 1.87.

GRAPHS AND CHARTS

On the test you'll need to both read graphs and determine what kinds of graphs are appropriate for different situations.

These questions require you to interpret information from graphs and charts; they will be pretty straightforward as long as you pay careful attention to detail. There are several different graph and chart types that may appear on the CBEST.

Bar Graphs

BAR GRAPHS present the numbers of an item that exist in different categories. The categories are shown on the one axis, and the number of items is shown on the other axis. Bar graphs are usually used to easily compare amounts.

Examples

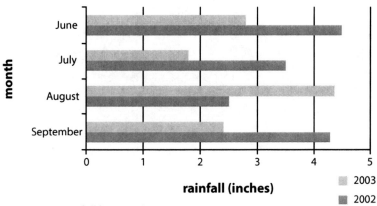

Figure 3.1. Rainfall by Month

The chart above shows rainfall in inches per month. Which month had the least amount of rainfall? Which had the most?

The shortest bar represents the month with the least rain, and the longest bar represents the month with the most rain: **July 2003 had the least**, and **June 2002 had the most**.

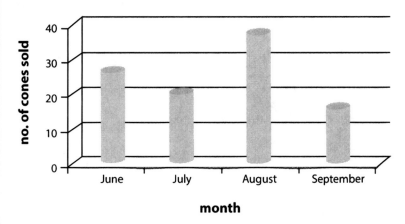

Figure 3.2. Ice Cream Cones Sold Per Month

Using the chart above, how many more ice cream cones were made in July than in September?

Tracing from the top of each bar to the scale on the left shows that sales in July were 20 and September sales were 15. So, **5 more cones were sold in July**.

CONTINUE

Pie Charts

Pie charts present parts of a whole, and are often used with percentages. Together, all the slices of the pie add up to the total number of items, or 100%.

Examples

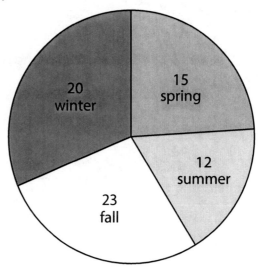

Figure 3.3. Birthdays by Season

The pie chart above shows the distribution of birthdays in a class of students. How many students have birthdays in the spring or summer?

Fifteen students have birthdays in spring and 12 in winter, so there are **27 students** with birthdays in spring or summer.

Using the same chart in the example before, what percentage of students have birthdays in winter?

Use the equation for percent:

$$percent = \frac{part}{whole} = \frac{winter\ birthdays}{total\ birthdays} =$$
$$\frac{20}{20 + 15 + 23 + 12} = \frac{20}{70} = \frac{2}{7} =$$
.286 or **28.6%**

Line Graphs

Line graphs show trends over time. The number of each item represented by the graph will be on the *y*-axis, and time will be on the *x*-axis.

Examples

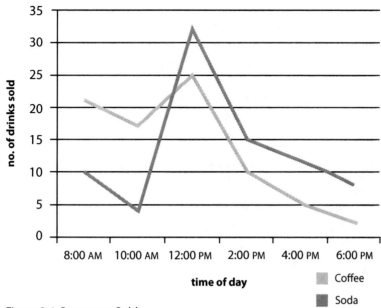

Figure 3.4. Beverages Sold

The line graph above shows beverage sales at an airport snack shop throughout the day. Which beverage sold more at 4:00 p.m.?

> At 4:00 p.m., approximately 12 sodas and 5 coffees were sold, so more **soda** was sold.

At what time of day were the most beverages sold?

> This question is asking for the time of day with the most sales of coffee and soda combined. It is not necessary to add up sales at each time of day to find the answer. Just from looking at the graph, you can see that sales for both beverages were highest at noon, so the answer must be **12:00 p.m**.

PROBABILITY

PROBABILITY is the likelihood that an event will take place. This likelihood is expressed as a value between 0 and 1. The closer the probability is to zero, the less likely the event is to occur; the closer the probability is to 1, the more likely it is to occur.

Probability of a Single Event

A probability is found by dividing the number of desired outcomes by the number of total possible outcomes. As with percentages, a probability is the ratio of a part to a whole, with the whole being the total number of things that could happen, and the part being the number of those things that would be considered a success. Probabilities can be written using percentages (40%), decimals (0.4), fractions $\left(\frac{2}{5}\right)$, or words (probability is 2 in 5).

CONTINUE

Examples

A bag holds 3 blue marbles, 5 green marbles, and 7 red marbles. If you pick one marble from the bag, what is the probability it will be blue?

> Because there are 15 marbles in the bag (3 + 5 + 7), the total number of possible outcomes is 15. Of those outcomes, 3 would be blue marbles, which is the desired outcome. With that information you can set up an equation:
>
> $probability = \frac{desired\ outcomes}{total\ possible\ outcomes} = \frac{3}{15} = \frac{1}{5}$
>
> The probability is **1 in 5 or 0.2 that a blue marble is picked.**

A bag contains 75 balls. If the probability that a ball selected from the bag will be red is 0.6, how many red balls are in the bag?

> Because you're solving for desired outcomes (the number of red balls), first you need to rearrange the equation:
>
> $probability = \frac{desired\ outcomes}{total\ possible\ outcomes} \rightarrow$
>
> $desired\ outcomes = probability \times total\ possible\ outcomes$
>
> In this problem, the desired outcome is choosing a red ball, and the total possible outcomes are represented by the 75 total balls.
>
> $desired\ outcomes = 0.6 \times 75 = 45$
>
> There are **45 red balls in the bag.**

A theater has 230 seats: 75 seats are in the orchestra area, 100 seats are in the mezzanine, and 55 seats are in the balcony. If a ticket is selected at random, what is the probability that it will be for either a mezzanine or balcony seat?

> In this problem, the desired outcome is a seat in either the mezzanine or balcony area and the total possible outcomes are represented by the 230 total seats, so the equation should be written as:
>
> $probability = \frac{desired\ outcomes}{total\ possible\ outcomes} = \frac{100 + 55}{230} = \textbf{0.67}$

The probability of selecting a student whose name begins with the letter *S* from a school attendance log is 7%. If there are 42 students whose names begin with *S* enrolled at the school, how many students attend the school?

> Because you're solving for total possible outcomes (total number of students), first you need to rearrange the equation:
>
> $total\ possible\ outcomes = \frac{desired\ outcomes}{probability}$
>
> In this problem, you are given a probability (7% or 0.07) and the number of desired outcomes (42). These can be plugged into the equation to solve:
>
> $total\ possible\ outcomes = \frac{42}{0.07} = \textbf{600 students}$

PART II: READING

50 questions

The reading section of the CBEST includes fifty multiple choice questions that will require you to analyze a variety of informational sources, including passages, graphs, tables, and tables of contents. The questions will cover topics from social sciences, humanities, health, and consumer affairs, but no specialized knowledge is required; you'll be relying only on the information given on the exam.

The length of reading selections will vary. Passages will be anywhere from a couple of sentences to a several hundred words in length. Long passages will include more questions than do short passages, although all passages will include anywhere from one to five questions. The questions will cover a variety of topics. You will be asked to:

- Identify the main idea of the passage.
- Identify the author's tone, attitude, opinion, or perspective.
- Recognize the author's intended audience.
- Find examples, details, and facts that support an author's claim.
- Choose statements that will strengthen or weaken the author's claims.
- Differentiate between fact and opinion in the passage.
- Summarize or paraphrase the information in the passage.
- Determine the meaning of underlined words using context clues in the passage.
- Identify words and phrases that help transition between ideas in the passage.
- Make an inference based on information in the passage.
- Identify how a passage is organized.
- Locate in a book, chapter, or article where specific information can be found.
- Form conclusions supported by the information presented in a table or graph.

The CBEST Reading section will require you to read both non-fiction and fiction passages and then answer questions about them. These questions will fall into three main categories:

ABOUT THE AUTHOR: The question will ask about the author's attitude, thoughts, and opinions. When encountering a question asking specifically about the author, pay attention to context clues in the article. The answer may not be explicitly stated but instead conveyed in the overall message.

PASSAGE FACTS: You must distinguish between facts and opinions presented in the passage. You may also be asked to identify specific information supplied by the author of the passage.

ADDITIONAL INFORMATION: These questions will have you look at what kind of information could be added to or was missing from the passage. They may also ask in what direction the passage was going. Questions may ask what statement could be added to strengthen the author's statement, or weaken it; they may also provide a fill-in-the-blank option to include a statement that is missing from, but fits with the rest of, the passage.

The Reading section will also include informational source comprehension questions. These questions don't refer back to a text passage; instead, they will ask you to interpret an informational source like a table of contents or book index.

STRATEGIES

Despite the different types of questions you will face, there are some strategies for Reading Comprehension which apply across the board:

- Read the answer choices first, then read the passage. This will save you time, as you will know what to look out for as you read.
- Use the process of elimination. Some answer choices are obviously incorrect and are relatively easy to detect. After reading the passage, eliminate those blatantly incorrect answer choices; this increases your chance of finding the correct answer much more quickly.
- Avoid negative statements. Generally, test-makers will not make negative statements about anyone or anything. Statements will be either neutral or positive, so if it seems like an answer choice has a negative connotation, it is very likely that the answer is false.

4

READING PASSAGES

THE MAIN IDEA

The main idea of a text is the purpose behind why a writer would choose to write a book, article, story, etc. Being able to find and understand the main idea is a critical skill necessary to comprehend and appreciate what you're reading.

Imagine that you're at a friend's home for the evening. He says, "Hey, I think we should watch this movie tonight. Is that ok with you?"

"Yeah, that sounds good," you reply. "What's it about?"

You'd like to know a little about what you'll be watching, but your question may not get you a satisfactory answer, because you've only asked about the topic of the film. The TOPIC—what the movie is about—is only half the story. Think, for example, about all the alien invasion films ever been made. While these films may share the same general subject, what they have to say about the aliens or about humanity's theoretical response to invasion may be very different. Each filmmaker has different ideas or opinions she wants to convey about a topic, just as writers write because they have something to say about a particular topic. When you look beyond the facts to the argument the writer is making about his topic, you're looking for the MAIN IDEA.

One more quick note: the CBEST may also ask about a passage's THEME, which is similar to, but distinct from its topic. While a topic is usually a specific *person, place, thing,* or *issue,* the theme is an *idea* or *concept* that the author refers back to frequently. Examples of common themes include ideas like the importance of family, the dangers of technology, and the beauty of nature.

There will be many questions on the CBEST that require you to differentiate between the topic, theme, and main idea of a passage. Let's look at an example passage to see how you would answer these questions.

TOPIC: The subject of the passage.

THEME: An idea or concept the author refers to repeatedly.

MAIN IDEA: The argument the writer is making about the topic.

Babe Didrikson Zaharias, one of the most decorated female athletes of the twentieth century, is an inspiration for everyone. Born in 1911 in Beaumont, Texas, Zaharias lived in a time when women were considered second-class to men, but she never let that stop her from becoming a champion. Babe was one of seven children in a poor immigrant family, and was competitive from an early age. As a child she excelled at most things she tried, especially sports, which continued into high school and beyond. After high school, Babe played amateur basketball for two years, and soon after began training in track and field. Despite the fact that women were only allowed to enter in three events, Babe represented the United States in the 1932 Los Angeles Olympics, and won two gold medals and one silver for track and field events.

In the early 1930s, Babe began playing golf which earned her a legacy. The first tournament she entered was a men's only tournament, however she did not make the cut to play. Playing golf as an amateur was the only option for a woman at this time, since there was no professional women's league. Babe played as an amateur for a little over a decade, until she turned pro in 1947 for the Ladies Professional Golf Association (LPGA) of which she was a founding member. During her career as a golfer, Babe won eighty-two tournaments, amateur and professional, including the U.S. Women's Open, All-American Open, and British Women's Open Golf Tournament. In 1953, Babe was diagnosed with cancer, but fourteen weeks later, she played in a tournament. That year she won her third U.S. Women's Open. However by 1955, she didn't have the physicality to compete anymore, and she died of the disease in 1956.

The topic of this paragraph is obviously Babe Zaharias—the whole passage describes events from her life. But what is the main idea of this paragraph? You might be tempted to answer, *Babe Zaharias*, or *Babe Zaharias' life*. Yes, Babe Zaharias' life is the topic of the passage—who or what the passage is about—but the topic is not the main idea. The main idea is what the writer wants to say about this subject. What is the writer saying about Babe Zaharias' life? She's saying that she's someone to admire—that's the main idea and what unites all the information in the paragraph. Lastly, what might the theme of the passage be? The writer refers to several broad concepts, including never giving up and overcoming the odds, both of which could be themes for the passage.

The example above shows two important traits of a main idea:
- It is general enough to encompass all of the ideas in the passage. The main idea of a passage should be broad enough for all of the other sentences in that passage to fit underneath it, like people under an umbrella.

- It asserts a specific viewpoint that the author supports with facts, opinions, or other details. In other words, the main idea takes a stand.

Examples

From so far away it's easy to imagine the surface of our solar system's planets as enigmas—how could we ever know what those far-flung planets really look like? It turns out, however, that scientists have a number of tools at their disposal that allow them to paint detailed pictures of many planets' surfaces. The topography of Venus, for example, has been explored by several space probes, including the Russian Venera landers and NASA's Magellan orbiter. These craft used imaging and radar to map the surface of the planet, identifying a whole host of features including volcanoes, craters, and a complex system of channels. Mars has similarly been mapped by space probes, including the famous Mars Rovers, which are automated vehicles that actually landed on the surface of Mars. These rovers have been used by NASA and other space agencies to study the geology, climate, and possible biology of the planet.

In addition these long-range probes, NASA has also used its series of orbiting telescopes to study distant planets. These four massively powerful telescopes include the famous Hubble Space Telescope as well as the Compton Gamma Ray Observatory, Chandra X-Ray Observatory, and the Spitzer Space Telescope. Scientists can use these telescopes to examine planets using not only visible light but also infrared and near-infrared light, ultraviolet light, x-rays and gamma rays.

Powerful telescopes aren't just found in space: NASA makes use of Earth-bound telescopes as well. Scientists at the National Radio Astronomy Observatory in Charlottesville, VA, have spent decades using radio imaging to build an incredibly detailed portrait of Venus' surface. In fact, Earth-bound telescopes offer a distinct advantage over orbiting telescopes because they allow scientists to capture data from a fixed point, which in turn allows them to effectively compare data collected over long period of time.

Which of the following sentences best describes the main idea of the passage?

A) It's impossible to know what the surfaces of other planets are really like.

B) Telescopes are an important tool for scientists studying planets in our solar system.

C) Venus' surface has many of the same features as the Earth's, including volcanoes, craters, and channels.

D) Scientists use a variety of advanced technologies to study the surface of the planets in our solar system.

Answer A) can be eliminated because it directly contradicts the rest of the passage. Answers B) and C) can also be eliminated because they offer only specific details from the passage—while both choices contain details from the passage, neither is general enough to encompass the passage as a whole. Only answer D) provides an assertion that is both backed up by the passage's content and general enough to cover the entire passage.

Topic and Summary Sentences

Writers sometimes lead with preliminary sentences that give the reader clear ideas of what the text is about. A sentence that encompasses the main idea of the text is the TOPIC SENTENCE.

Notice, for example, how the first sentence in the example paragraph about Babe Zaharias states the main idea: *Babe Didrikson Zaharias, one of the most decorated female athletes of the twentieth century, is an inspiration for everyone.*

Topic sentences are often found at the beginning of paragraphs. Sometimes, though, writers begin with specific supporting details and lead up to the main idea; in this case the topic sentence is found at the end of the paragraph. In other cases there isn't a clear topic sentence at all—but that doesn't mean there isn't a main idea; the author has just chosen not to express it in a clear topic sentence. You may also see a SUMMARY SENTENCE at the end of a passage. As its name suggests, this sentence sums up the passage, often by restating the main idea and the author's key evidence supporting it.

Example

In the following paragraph, what are the topic and summary sentences?

The Constitution of the United States establishes a series of limits to rein in centralized power. Separation of powers distributes federal authority among three competing branches: the executive, the legislative, and the judicial. Checks and balances allow the branches to check the usurpation of power by any one branch. States' rights are protected under the Constitution from too much encroachment by the federal government. Enumeration of powers names the specific and few powers the federal government has. These four restrictions have helped sustain the American republic for over two centuries.

The topic sentence is the first sentence in the paragraph. It introduces the topic of discussion, in this case the constitutional limits aimed at resisting centralized power. The summary sentence is the last sentence in the paragraph. It sums up the information that was just presented: here, that constitutional limits have helped sustain the United States of America for over two hundred years.

Implied Main Idea

When there's no clear topic sentence, you're looking for an IMPLIED MAIN IDEA. This requires some detective work: you will need to look at the author's word choice and tone in addition to the content of the passage to find his or her main idea. Let's look at an example paragraph.

Examples

One of my summer reading books was Mockingjay. Though it's several hundred pages long, I read it in just a few days. I couldn't wait to see what happened to Katniss, the main character. But by the time I got to the end, I wondered if I should have spent my week doing something else. The ending was such a letdown that I completely forgot that I'd enjoyed most of the book.

There's no topic sentence here, but you should still be able to find the main idea. Look carefully at what the writer says and how she says it. What is she suggesting?

A) *Mockingjay* is a terrific novel.

B) *Mockingjay* is disappointing.

C) *Mockingjay* is full of suspense.

D) *Mockingjay* is a lousy novel.

Understanding the tone of a passage can help you quickly eliminate answer choices.

The correct answer is B): the novel is disappointing. How can you tell that this is the main idea? First, you can eliminate choice C) because it's too specific to be a main idea. It only deals with one specific aspect of the novel (its suspense).

Sentences A), B), and D), on the other hand, all express a larger idea about the quality of the novel. However, only one of these statements can actually serve as a "net" for the whole paragraph. Notice that while the first few sentences praise the novel, the last two criticize it. Clearly, this is a mixed review.

Therefore, the best answer is B). Sentence A) is too positive and doesn't account for the "letdown" of an ending. Sentence D), on the other hand, is too negative and doesn't account for the reader's sense of suspense and interest in the main character. But sentence B) allows for both positive and negative aspects— when a good thing turns bad, we often feel disappointed.

Fortunately, none of Alyssa's coworkers has ever seen inside the large filing drawer in her desk. Disguised by the meticulous neatness of the rest of her workspace, there was no sign of the chaos beneath. To even open it, she had to struggle for several minutes with the enormous pile of junk jamming the drawer, until it would suddenly give way, and papers, folders, and candy wrappers spilled out of the top and onto the floor. It was an organizational nightmare, with torn notes and spreadsheets haphazardly thrown on top of each other, and melted candy smeared across pages. She was worried the odor would soon permeate to her coworker's desks, revealing to them her secret.

Which of the following expresses the main idea of this paragraph?

A) Alyssa wishes she could move to a new desk.

B) Alyssa wishes she had her own office.

C) Alyssa is glad none of her coworkers know about her messy drawer.

D) Alyssa is sad because she doesn't have any coworkers.

What the paragraph adds up to is that Alyssa is terribly embarrassed about her messy drawer, and she's glad that none of her coworkers have seen it, making C) the correct answer choice. This is the main idea. The paragraph opens with the word *fortunately*, so we know that she thinks it's a good thing that none of her coworkers have seen inside the drawer. Plus, notice how the drawer is described: *it was an organizational nightmare*, and it apparently doesn't even function properly: *to even open the drawer, she had to struggle for several minutes*. The writer reveals that it has an odor, with *melted candy* inside. Alyssa is clearly ashamed of her drawer and worries about what her coworkers would think if they saw inside it.

SUPPORTING DETAILS

SUPPORTING DETAILS provide more support for the author's main idea. For instance, in the Babe Zaharias example, the writer makes the general assertion that *Babe Didrikson Zaharias, one of the most decorated female athletes of the twentieth century, is an inspiration for everyone*. The other sentences offer specific facts and details that prove why Babe Zaharias is an inspiration: the struggles she faced as a female athlete, and the specific years she competed in th Olympics and in golf.

Writers often provide clues that can help you identify supporting details. These SIGNAL WORDS tell you that a supporting fact or idea will follow, and so can be helpful in identifying supporting details. Signal words can also help you rule out sentences that are not the main idea or topic sentence: if a sentence begins with one of these phrases, it will likely be too specific to be a main idea.

Questions on the CBEST will ask you to do two things with supporting details: you will need to find details that support a particular idea and also explain why a particular detail was included in the passage. In order to answer these questions, you need to have a solid understanding of the passage's main idea. With this knowledge, you can determine how a supporting detail fits in with the larger structure of the passage.

SIGNAL WORDS
- for example
- specifically
- in addition
- furthermore
- for instance
- others
- in particular
- some

Examples

From so far away it's easy to imagine the surface of our solar system's planets as enigmas—how could we ever know what those far-flung planets really look like? It turns out, however, that scientists have a number of tools at their disposal that allow them to paint detailed pictures of many planets' surfaces. The topography of Venus, for example, has been explored by several space probes, including the Russian Venera landers and NASA's Magellan orbiter. These crafts used imaging and radar to map the surface of the planet, identifying a whole host of features including volcanoes, craters, and a complex system of channels. Mars has similarly been mapped by space probes, including the famous Mars Rovers, which are automated vehicles that actually landed on the surface of Mars. These rovers have been used by NASA and other space agencies to study the geology, climate, and possible biology of the planet.

In addition to these long-range probes, NASA has also used its series of orbiting telescopes to study distant planets. These four massively powerful telescopes include the famous Hubble Space Telescope as well as the Compton Gamma Ray Observatory, Chandra X-Ray Observatory, and the Spitzer Space Telescope. Scientists can use these telescopes to examine planets using not only visible light but also infrared and near-infrared light, ultraviolet light, x-rays and gamma rays.

Powerful telescopes aren't just found in space: NASA makes use of Earth-bound telescopes as well. Scientists at the National Radio Astronomy Observatory in Charlottesville, VA, have spent decades using radio imaging to build an incredibly detailed portrait of Venus' surface. In fact, Earth-bound telescopes offer a distinct advantage over orbiting telescopes because they allow scientists to capture data from a fixed point, which in turn allows them to effectively compare data collected over long period of time.

Which sentence from the text best helps develop the idea that scientists make use of many different technologies to study the surfaces of other planets?

A)   These rovers have been used by NASA and other space agencies to study the geology, climate, and possible biology of the planet.

B)   From so far away it's easy to imagine the surface of our solar system's planets as enigmas—how could we ever know what those far-flung planets really look like?

C)   In addition these long-range probes, NASA has also used its series of orbiting telescopes to study distant planets.

D)   These crafts used imaging and radar to map the surface of the planet, identifying a whole host of features including volcanoes, craters, and a complex system of channels.

You're looking for detail from the passage that supports the main idea—scientists make use of many different technologies to study the surfaces of other planets. Answer A) includes a specific detail about rovers, but does not offer any details that support the idea of multiple technologies being used. Similarly, answer D) provides another specific detail about space probes. Answer B) doesn't provide any supporting details; it simply introduces the topic of the passage. Only answer C) provides a detail that directly supports the author's assertion that scientists use multiple technologies to study the planets.

$\longrightarrow$
CONTINUE

If true, which detail could be added to the passage above to support the author's argument that scientists use many different technologies to study the surface of planets?

A) Because the Earth's atmosphere blocks x-rays, gamma rays, and infrared radiation, NASA needed to put telescopes in orbit above the atmosphere.

B) In 2015, NASA released a map of Venus which was created by compiling images from orbiting telescopes and long-range space probes.

C) NASA is currently using the Curiosity and Opportunity rovers to look for signs of ancient life on Mars.

D) NASA has spent over $2.5 billion to build, launch, and repair the Hubble Space Telescope.

You can eliminate answers C) and D) because they don't address the topic of studying the surface of planets. Answer A) can also be eliminated because it only addresses a single technology. Only choice B) provides would add support to the author's claim about the importance of using multiple technologies.

The author likely included the detail Earth-bound telescopes offer a distinct advantage over orbiting telescopes because they allow scientists to capture data from a fixed point in order to:

A) Explain why it has taken scientists so long to map the surface of Venus.

B) Suggest that Earth-bound telescopes are the most important equipment used by NASA scientists.

C) Prove that orbiting telescopes will soon be replaced by Earth-bound telescopes.

D) Demonstrate why NASA scientists rely on my different types of scientific equipment.

Only answer D) speaks directly to the author's main argument. The author doesn't mention how long it has taken to map the surface of Venus (answer A), nor does he say that one technology is more important than the others (answer B). And while this detail does highlight the advantages of using Earth-bound telescopes, the author's argument is that many technologies are being used at the same time, so there's no reason to think that orbiting telescopes will be replaced (answer C).

UNDERSTANDING THE AUTHOR

Author's Purpose

Whenever an author writes a text, she always has a purpose, whether that's to entertain, inform, explain, or persuade. A short story, for example, is meant to entertain, while an online news article would be designed to inform the public about a current event.

Each of these different types of writing has a specific name. On the exam, you may be asked to identify which of these categories a passage fits into either by name or by general purpose:

- Narrative writing tells a story (novel, short story, play).
- Expository writing informs people (newspaper and magazine articles).
- Technical writing explains something (product manual, directions).
- Persuasive writing tries to convince the reader of something (opinion column on a blog).

You may also be asked about primary and secondary sources. These terms describe not the writing itself but the author's relationship to the topic. A primary source is an unaltered piece of writing that was composed during the time when the events being described took place; these texts are often written by the people involved. A secondary source might address the same topic but provides extra commentary or analysis. These texts can be written by people not directly involved in the events. For example, a book written by a political candidate to inform people about his or her stand on an issue is a primary source; an online article written by a journalist analyzing how that position will affect the election is a secondary source.

Example

Elizabeth closed her eyes and braced herself on the armrests that divided her from her fellow passengers. Take-off was always the worst part for her. The revving of the engines, the way her stomach dropped as the plane lurched upward: it made her feel sick. Then, she had to watch the world fade away beneath her, getting smaller and smaller until it was just her and the clouds hurtling through the sky. Sometimes (but only sometimes) it just had to be endured, though. She focused on the thought of her sister's smiling face and her new baby nephew as the plane slowly pulled onto the runway.

The passage above is reflective of which type of writing?

A) narrative
B) expository
C) technical
D) persuasive

The passage is telling a story—we meet Elizabeth and learn about her fear of flying—so it's a narrative text. There is no factual information presented or explained, nor is the author trying to persuade the reader.

Audience

A good author will write with a specific audience in mind. For example, an opinion column on a website might be specifically targeted at undecided voters, or a brochure for an upcoming art exhibit might address people who have donated money to the museum in the past.

The author's audience can influence what information is included in the text, the tone the author uses, and the structure of the text.

The easiest way to identify the intended audience of a text is simply to ask yourself who would benefit the most from the information in the passage. A passage about how often to change the oil in a car would provide useful information to new drivers, but likely wouldn't tell an experienced driver something she didn't already know. Thus, the audience is likely new drivers who are learning to take care of cars.

The author may also directly or indirectly refer to his audience. The author of an article on oil changes might say something like new drivers will want to keep an eye on their mileage when deciding how often to get an oil change, which tells the reader who the intended audience is.

Example

The museum's newest exhibit opens today! The Ecology of the Colombia River Basin is an exciting collaboration between the New Valley Museum of Natural Science and the U.S. Department of the Interior. The exhibit includes plants, insects, birds, and mammals that are unique to the Colombia River Basin and explores the changes that have occurred in this delicate ecosystem over the last century. The exhibit is kid friendly, with interactive, hands-on exhibits and exciting audio-visual presentations. Individual tickets are available on the museum's website, and groups may apply for special ticket prices by calling the museum directly.

The intended audience for this passage likely includes all of the following except

A) a middle school biology teacher

B) employees of the U.S. Department of the Interior

C) parents of young children

D) naturalists with an interest in local birds

The passage provides information to anyone who might be interested in an exhibit on the ecology of the Colombia River Basin. This includes biology teachers (who can get special group ticket prices), parents of young children (who now know the exhibit is kid friendly), and naturalists (who will want to see the unique birds). The only people who would not learn anything new from reading the passage are employees of the U.S. Department of the Interior (answer B), who likely already know about the exhibit since they helped create it.

Tone

The author of a text expresses how she feels about her subject and audience through the tone of the text. For example, a newspaper article about a prominent philanthropist might have be serious and appreciative, while a website blurb about an upcoming sale could be playful and relaxed.

Table 5.1. Tone Words

POSITIVE	NEGATIVE	NEUTRAL
admiring	angry	casual
approving	annoyed	detached
celebratory	belligerent	formal
comforting	angry	impartial
confident	bitter	informal
earnest	condescending	objective
encouraging	confused	questioning
excited	cynical	unconcerned
forthright	depressed	
funny	derisive	
hopeful	despairing	
humorous	disrespectful	
modest	embarrassed	
nostalgic	fearful	
optimistic	gloomy	
playful	melancholy	
poignant	mournful	
proud	ominous	
relaxed	pessimistic	
respectful	skeptical	
sentimental	solemn	
silly	suspicious	
sympathetic	unsympathetic	

Authors signify tone in a number of ways. The main clue to look for is the author's diction, or word choice. Obviously, if the author is choosing words that have a negative connotation, then the overall tone of the text is negative, and words with a positive connotation will create a positive tone. For example, the author of a biographical article may choose to describe his subject as determined or pigheaded; both mean similar things, but the first has a more positive connotation than the second. Literary devices such as imagery and metaphors can similarly create a specific tone by evoking feeling in the reader.

Example

It could be said that the great battle between the North and South, the Civil War, was a battle for individual identity. The states of the South had their own culture, one based on farming, independence, and the rights of both man and state to determine their own paths. Similarly, the North had forged its own identity as a center of centralized commerce and manufacturing. This clash of lifestyles was bound to create tension, and this tension was bound to lead to war. But people who try to sell you this narrative are wrong.

CONTINUE

The tone of the passage above can best be described as

A) formal and forthright

B) casual and mournful

C) detached and solemn

D) objective and skeptical

The author of this passage is using a formal tone as indicated by his use of academic-sounding phrases like *rights of both man and state* and *centralize commerce*. He is also very forthright in his final sentence, when he directly states his opinion to the reader, so the correct answer is A). Because of the formal language, the tone isn't casual, and the author's obvious strong feelings about the topic eliminate *detached* and *objective* as answer choices. The author's tone could be described as skeptical, however answer D) has already been eliminated.

TEXT STRUCTURE

Authors can structure passages in a number of different ways. These distinct organizational patterns, referred to as text structure, use the logical relationships between ideas to improve the readability and coherence of a text. The most common ways passages are organized include:

- problem-solution: the author presents a problem and then discusses a solution
- comparison-contrast: the author presents two situations and then discusses the similarities and differences
- cause-effect: the author presents an action and then discusses the resulting effects
- descriptive: an idea, object, person, or other item is described in detail

Example

The issue of public transportation has begun to haunt the fast-growing cities of the southern United States. Unlike their northern counterparts, cities like Atlanta, Dallas, and Houston have long promoted growth out and not up—these are cities full of sprawling suburbs and single-family homes, not densely concentrated skyscrapers and apartments. What to do then, when all those suburbanites need to get into the central business districts for work? For a long time it seemed highways were the twenty-lane wide expanses of concrete that would allow commuters to move from home to work and back again. But these modern miracles have become time-sucking, pollution spewing nightmares. They may not like it, but it's time for these cities to turn toward public transport like trains and buses if they want their cities to remain livable.

The organization of this passage can best be described as:

A) a comparison of two similar ideas

B) a description of a place

C) a discussion of several effects all related to the same cause

D) a discussion of a problem followed by the suggestion of a solution

You can exclude answer choice C) because the author provides no root cause or a list of effects. From there this question gets tricky, because the passage contains structures similar to those described above. For example, it compares two things (cities in the North and South) and describes a place (a sprawling city). However, if you look at the overall organization of the passage, you can see that it starts by presenting a problem (transportation) and then presents a solution (trains and buses), making answer D) the only choice that encompasses the entire passage.

FACTS VS. OPINIONS

On CBEST Reading passages you might be asked to identify a statement in a passage as either a fact or an opinion, so you'll need to know the difference between the two. A **FACT** is a statement or thought that can be proven to be true. The statement *Wednesday comes after Tuesday* is a fact—you can point to a calendar to prove it. In contrast, an **opinion** is an assumption that is not based in fact and cannot be proven to be true. The assertion that *television is more entertaining than feature films* is an opinion—people will disagree on this, and there's no reference you can use to prove or disprove it.

Which of the following words would be associated with opinions?
- for example . . .
- studies have shown . . .
- I believe . . .
- in fact . . .
- the best/worst . . .
- it's possible that . .

Example

Exercise is critical for healthy development in children. Today, there is an epidemic of unhealthy children in the United States who will face health problems in adulthood due to poor diet and lack of exercise as children. This is a problem for all Americans, especially with the rising cost of healthcare.

It is vital that school systems and parents encourage their children to engage in a minimum of thirty minutes of cardiovascular exercise each day, mildly increasing their heart rate for a sustained period. This is proven to decrease the likelihood of developmental diabetes, obesity, and a multitude of other health problems. Also, children need a proper diet rich in fruits and vegetables so that they can grow and develop physically, as well as learn healthy eating habits early on.

CONTINUE

Keep an eye out for answer choices that may be facts, but which are not stated or discussed in the passage.

Which of the following is a fact in the passage, not an opinion?

A) Fruits and vegetables are the best way to help children be healthy.

B) Children today are lazier than they were in previous generations.

C) The risk of diabetes in children is reduced by physical activity.

D) Children should engage in thirty minutes of exercise a day.

Choice B) can be discarded immediately because it is negative and is not discussed anywhere in the passage. Answers A) and D) are both opinions—the author is promoting exercise, fruits, and vegetables as a way to make children healthy. (Notice that these incorrect answers contain words that hint at being an opinion such as *best, should,* or other comparisons.) Answer B), on the other hand, is a simple fact stated by the author; it's introduced by the word *proven* to indicate that you don't need to just take the author's word for it.

DRAWING CONCLUSIONS

In addition to understanding the main idea and factual content of a passage, you'll also be asked to take your analysis one step further and anticipate what other information could logically be added to the passage. In a non-fiction passage, for example, you might be asked which statement the author of the passage would agree with. In an excerpt from a fictional work, you might be asked to anticipate what the character would do next.

To answer these questions, you need to have a solid understanding of the topic, theme, and main idea of the passage; armed with this information, you can figure out which of the answer choices best fits within those criteria (or alternatively, which ones do not). For example, if the author of the passage is advocating for safer working conditions in textile factories, any supporting details that would be added to the passage should support that idea. You might add sentences that contain information about the number of accidents that occur in textile factories or that outline a new plan for fire safety.

Examples

Today, there is an epidemic of unhealthy children in the United States who will face health problems in adulthood due to poor diet and lack of exercise during their childhood. This is a problem for all Americans, as adults with chronic health issues are adding to the rising cost of healthcare. A child who grows up living an unhealthy lifestyle is likely to become an adult who does the same.

Because exercise is critical for healthy development in children, it is vital that school systems and parents encourage their children to engage in a minimum of thirty minutes of cardiovascular exercise each day. Even this small amount of exercise has been proven to decrease the likelihood that young people will develop diabetes, obesity, and other health issues as adults. In addition to exercise, children need a proper diet rich in fruits and vegetables so that they can grow and develop physically. Starting a good diet early also teaches children healthy eating habits they will carry into adulthood.

The author of this passage would most likely agree with which statement?

A) Parents are solely responsible for the health of their children.

B) Children who do not want to exercise should not be made to.

C) Improved childhood nutrition will help lower the amount Americans spend on healthcare.

D) It's not important to teach children healthy eating habits because they will learn them as adults.

The author would most likely support answer C): he mentions in the first paragraph that unhealthy habits are adding to the rising cost of healthcare. The main idea of the passage is that nutrition and exercise are important for children, so answer B) doesn't make sense—the author would likely support measures to encourage children to exercise. Answers A) and D) can also be eliminated because they are directly contradicted in the text. The author specifically mentions the role of schools systems, so he doesn't believe parents are solely responsible for their children's health. He also specifically states that children who grow up with unhealthy habit will become adults with unhealthy habits, which contradicts D).

Elizabeth closed her eyes and braced herself on the armrests that divided her from her fellow passengers. Take-off was always the worst part for her. The revving of the engines, the way her stomach dropped as the plane lurched upward: it made her feel sick. Then, she had to watch the world fade away beneath her, getting smaller and smaller until it was just her and the clouds hurtling through the sky. Sometimes (but only sometimes) it just had to be endured, though. She focused on the thought of her sister's smiling face and her new baby nephew as the plane slowly pulled onto the runway.

Which of the following is Elizabeth least likely to do in the future?

A) Take a flight to her brother's wedding.

B) Apply for a job as a flight attendant.

C) Never board an airplane again.

D) Get sick on an airplane.

It's clear from the passage that Elizabeth hates flying, but it willing to endure it for the sake of visiting her family. Thus, it seems likely that she would be willing to get on a plane for her brother's wedding, making A) and C) incorrect answers. The passage also explicitly tells us that she feels sick on planes, so D) is likely to happen. We can infer, though, that she would not enjoy being on an airplane for work, so she's very unlikely to apply for a job as a flight attendant, which is choice B).

CONTINUE

MEANING OF WORDS AND PHRASES

On the Reading section you may also be asked to provide definitions or intended meanings for words within passages. You may have never encountered some of these words before the test, but there are tricks you can use to figure out what they mean.

Context Clues

The most fundamental vocabulary skill is using the context in which a word is used to determine its meaning. Your ability to observe sentences closely is extremely useful when it comes to understanding new vocabulary words.

There are two types of context that can help you understand the meaning of unfamiliar words: situational context and sentence context. Regardless of which context is present, these types of questions are not really testing your knowledge of vocabulary; rather, they test your ability to comprehend the meaning of a word through its usage.

SITUATIONAL CONTEXT is context that is presented by the setting or circumstances in which a word or phrase occurs. SENTENCE CONTEXT occurs within the specific sentence that contains the vocabulary word. To figure out words using sentence context clues, you should first determine the most important words in the sentence.

There are four types of clues that can help you understand context, and therefore the meaning of a word:

- RESTATEMENT clues occur when the definition of the word is clearly stated in the sentence.
- POSITIVE/NEGATIVE CLUES can tell you whether a word has a positive or negative meaning.
- CONTRAST CLUES include the opposite meaning of a word. Words like *but, on the other hand,* and *however* are tip-offs that a sentence contains a contrast clue.
- SPECIFIC DETAIL CLUES provide a precise detail that can help you understand the meaning of the word.

It is important to remember that more than one of these clues can be present in the same sentence. The more there are, the easier it will be to determine the meaning of the word. For example, the following sentence uses both restatement and positive/negative clues: *Janet suddenly found herself destitute, so poor she could barely afford to eat.* The second part of the sentence clearly indicates that *destitute* is a negative word. It also restates the meaning: very poor.

Examples

I had a hard time reading her *illegible* handwriting.

A) neat

B) unsafe

C) sloppy

D) educated

Already, you know that this sentence is discussing something that is hard to read. Look at the word that illegible is describing: handwriting. Based on context clues, you can tell that illegible means that her handwriting is hard to read.

Next, look at the answer choices. Choice A), *neat,* is obviously a wrong answer because neat handwriting would not be difficult to read. Choices B) and D), *unsafe* and *educated,* don't make sense. Therefore, choice C), *sloppy,* is the best answer.

The dog was *dauntless* in the face of danger, braving the fire to save the girl trapped inside the building.

A) difficult

B) fearless

C) imaginative

D) startled

Demonstrating bravery in the face of danger would be B) fearless. In this case, the restatement clue (braving the fire) tells you exactly what the word means.

Beth did not spend any time preparing for the test, but Tyrone kept a *rigorous* study schedule.

A) strict

B) loose

C) boring

D) strange

In this case, the contrast word *but* tells us that Tyrone studied in a different way than Beth, which means it's a contrast clue. If Beth did not study hard, then Tyrone did. The best answer, therefore, is choice A).

Analyzing Words

As you no doubt know, determining the meaning of a word can be more complicated than just looking in a dictionary. A word might have more than one DENOTATION, or definition; which one the author intends can only be judged by looking at the surrounding text. For example, the word *quack* can refer to the sound a duck makes, or to a person who publicly pretends to have a qualification which he or she does not actually possess.

A word may also have different CONNOTATIONS, which are the implied meanings and emotion a word evokes in the reader. For example, a cubicle is a simply a walled desk in an office, but for many the word implies a constrictive, uninspiring workplace. Connotations can vary greatly between cultures and even between individuals.

Lastly, authors might make use of FIGURATIVE LANGUAGE, which is the use of a word to imply something other than the word's literal definition. This is often done by comparing two things. If you say *I felt like a butterfly when I got a new haircut*, the listener knows you don't resemble an insect but instead felt beautiful and transformed.

Word Structure

Although you are not expected to know every word in the English language for your test, you will need the ability to use deductive reasoning to find the choice that is the best match for the word in question, which is why we are going to explain how to break a word into its parts to determine its meaning. Many words can be broken down into three main parts:

PREFIX — ROOT — SUFFIX

ROOTS are the building blocks of all words. Every word is either a root itself or has a root. Just as a plant cannot grow without roots, neither can vocabulary, because a word must have a root to give it meaning. The root is what is left when you strip away all the prefixes and suffixes from a word. For example, in the word *unclear*, if you take away the prefix *un-*, you have the root *clear*.

Roots are not always recognizable words, because they generally come from Latin or Greek words, such as *nat*, a Latin root meaning born. The word *native*, which means a person born in a referenced placed, comes from this root, so does the word *prenatal*, meaning before birth. It's important to keep in mind, however, that roots do not always match the exact definitions of words, and they can have several different spellings.

PREFIXES are syllables added to the beginning of a word and **SUFFIXES** are syllables added to the end of the word. Both carry assigned meanings and can be attached to a word to completely change the word's meaning or to enhance the word's original meaning.

Let's use the word prefix itself as an example: *fix* means to place something securely and *pre-* means before. Therefore, *prefix* means to place something before or in front. Now let's look at a suffix: in the word *feminism*, *femin* is a root which means female. The suffix *-ism* means act, practice, or process. Thus, *feminism* is the process of establishing equal rights for women.

Although you cannot determine the meaning of a word by a prefix or suffix alone, you can use this knowledge to eliminate answer choices; understanding whether the word is positive or negative can give you the partial meaning of the word.

Can you figure out the definition of the following words using their parts?
- ambidextrous
- anthropology
- egocentric
- diagram
- hemisphere
- homicide
- metamorphosis
- nonsense
- portable
- rewind
- submarine
- triangle
- unicycle

5

INFORMATIONAL SOURCE COMPREHENSION

On the CBEST exam, you will encounter questions designed to test your comprehension of sources that convey all sorts of information. These sources may be visual (e.g. graphs) or textual (e.g., table of contents, indexes).

INDEXES AND TABLES OF CONTENTS

An **INDEX** is an alphabetical list of topics, and their associated page numbers, covered in a text. A **TABLE OF CONTENTS** is an outline of a text that includes topics and page numbers. Both of these can be used to look up information, but each has a slightly different purpose. An index helps the reader determine where in the text he or she can find specific details. A table of contents shows the reader the general arrangement of the text.

When would it be appropriate to use an index but not a table of contents?

Examples

Use the examples below to answer the following questions.

> Nursing, 189-296
> certification, 192-236
> code of ethics, 237-291
> Procedure, 34-55

According to the index above, where might the reader find information about the nursing code of ethics?

This information can be found from pages 237-291.

According to the table of contents above, in which chapter would the reader find information about the circumference of a circle?

The circumference of a circle is part of geometry, so that information would be found in Chapter 2.

HEADINGS AND SUBHEADINGS

In a long printed work, a general topic or subject is usually divided into categories and sections so the text can be easily navigated and read. A HEADING is a subcategory of the subject, and a SUBHEADING is a subcategory of a heading. Both types of headings preview what will be covered in their respective sections, but a heading usually encompasses a broader range of information than a subheading does. The font for headings is typically larger than the font for subheadings.

Examples

Use the example below to answer the following questions.

> **The Constitution of the United States of America**
>
> Article I
>
> Section I
>
> Section II
>
> Section III
>
> Section IV
>
> Section V

Is Article I a heading or subheading?

The subject is the Constitution of the United States of America. Since a heading is a subcategory of the subject, Article I is classified as a heading.

Is Section III a heading or subheading?

You already know that the subject is the Constitution of the United States of America. You also know that Article I is a heading. Since a subheading is a subcategory of a heading, Section III is classified as a subheading.

GRAPHIC REPRESENTATIONS OF INFORMATION

Information is usually represented as text, but it can also be represented graphically. Types of graphic information include charts, maps, graphs, drawings, and photographs. Graphic representations are used to quickly visualize an idea or compare bits of information. They are typically accompanied by a legend or additional information that aids comprehension.

Examples

Use the chart below to answer the following questions.

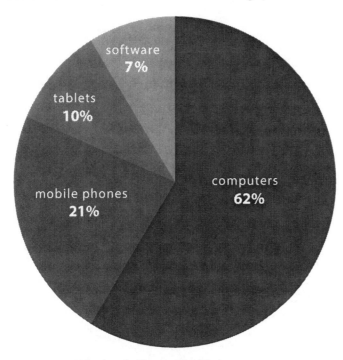

Figure 6.1. Wholesale Electronics' Sales

Which product accounts for most of Wholesale Electronics' total sales?

At sixty-two percent, computers account for most of Wholesale Electronics' total sales.

Mobile phones and tablets comprise what percentage of Wholesale Electronics' total sales?

Mobile phones and tablets comprise thirty-one percent of Wholesale Electronics' total sales.

PART III: WRITING

2 Essays

The Writing section of the CBEST requires you to complete two essays. There are no time restrictions for either of these essays, but plan to spend thirty to forty-five minutes on each. Although there are no wrong or right answers on these essays, they will be scored based on content and quality (i.e., they'll be scored based on how well you write, not the specific arguments you make). This means your essay must be logical and well-developed with a focused main idea and plenty of supporting details.

Each essay will be scored from 1 to 4, with 4 being the highest:

- Score of 4: This is a well-written essay that addresses the topic clearly and coherently; is free of errors; has a well-supported argument that includes additional information; incorporates an easy-to-read format; and uses accurate word choice.

- Score of 3: This is an essay that might have a few minor errors in syntax or punctuation, but those do not detract from the readers' ability to understand the meaning. The essay presents a reasonably clear argument, although supporting arguments could have been better.

- Score of 2: This is an essay that initially addresses the topic, but quickly loses focus and confuses the reader. Word choice is poor, and the essay includes multiple errors which are distracting. Supporting arguments are very weak and do not relate well to the topic.

- Score of 1: An essay scoring a 1 generally does not address the topic at all, immediately losing focus and clarity. It contains serious errors which are not only distracting, but also cause confusion for the reader. These essays either have a lack of supporting arguments, or the supporting arguments are irrelevant to the topic.

The first essay will be expository, meaning you'll be asked to take a stand on a particular issue and explain your reasoning. The second essay will ask you to write about a personal experience; the goal of this essay should be to express your own thoughts and feelings coherently and effectively. Below are two example outlines for how you might chose to structure these essays.

EXPOSITORY ESSAY

Paragraph 1	Introduce the issue, address the opposing viewpoints, and state your thesis.
Paragraph 2	Support your claim.
Paragraph 3-4	Provide further evidence and examples.
Paragraph 5	Explain your conclusion.

EXPRESSIVE ESSAY

Paragraph 1	Introduce the topic, provide any needed information, and state your thesis.
Paragraph 2	Describe any background information and events.
Paragraph 3	Describe the choices you needed to make relating to your experience.
Paragraph 4	Describe the results of your actions.
Paragraph 5	Explain your conclusion.

6

WRITING ESSAYS

When writing an essay, keep some specific things in mind in order to clearly communicate your idea. As you plan and draft your essay, be sure that you take a position, address complexities of the issue, put in specific ideas that help explain your position, and maintain an organized, logical structure. Also try to include varied sentence structures and vocabulary. The following sections walk through these steps and give you examples of what each looks like.

STRUCTURING THE ESSAY

There are many ways to organize an essay, and there are a few main things you can do to ensure that whatever structure you choose will work.

The first thing to realize is that there are many different kinds of essays. Each one has slightly different methods of delivering an idea, but they all have the same basic parts—introduction, body, and conclusion. The most common essay types are persuasive essays and expository essays. A persuasive essay takes a position on an issue and attempts to show the reader why it is correct. An expository essay explains different aspects of an issue without necessarily taking a side. Each of these essay types can be developed using various different methods.

Introductions
Use an introduction and a conclusion that frame your argument or idea. The introduction is a good place to bring up complexities, counterarguments, and context, all things that will help the reader understand why you chose the idea you did. In the conclusion, revisit those issues and wrap all of them up.

Example

Below is an example of an introduction for one of the thesis statements from the previous section. Note that it gives some context for the argument, acknowledges the opposite side, and gives the reader a good idea of what complexities the issue holds.

Technology has changed massively in the last several years, but today's generation barely notices—high school students today are experienced with the internet, computers, apps, cameras, cell phones, and all kinds of technology. Teenagers need to be taught to use all these things safely and responsibly. Opponents of 1:1 technology programs might argue that students will be distracted or misuse the technology, but that is exactly why schools and teachers must teach them to use it. By providing technology to students, schools can help them use it for things such as creating great projects with other students, keeping in touch with teachers and classmates, and researching for class projects. In a world where technology is improving and changing at a phenomenal rate, schools have a responsibility to teach students how to navigate that technology safely and effectively, and providing each student with a laptop or tablet is one way to help them do that.

The Body Paragraphs

Group similar ideas together and have a plan for paragraphs. You don't want to write one big chunk of a paragraph. Some ways to organize your essay include creating paragraphs that describe or explain each reason you give in your thesis; addressing the issue as a problem and offering a solution in a separate paragraph; telling a story that demonstrates your point (make sure to break it into paragraphs around related ideas); comparing and contrasting the merits of two opposing sides of the issue (make sure to draw a conclusion about which is better at the end).

Make sure that each paragraph is consistent inside— that there are no extra ideas that seem unrelated to the paragraph's main idea.

In the section entitled *Providing Supporting Evidence*, there is an example of a paragraph that is internally consistent and explains one of the main reasons given in one of the sample thesis statements above. Your essay should have one or more paragraphs like this to form the main body.

Conclusions

In order to end your essay smoothly, write a conclusion that reminds the reader why you were talking about these topics in the first place. Go back to the ideas in the introduction and thesis sentence, but be careful not to simply restate your ideas.

Example

Here is a sample conclusion paragraph that could go with the introduction written previously. Notice that this conclusion talks about the same topics as the introduction (changing technology and the responsibility of schools), but it does not simply rewrite the thesis.

As technology continues to change, teens will continue to need to adapt to it. Schools already teach people how to interact and fit into society, so it makes sense that they would also teach how to fit technology into the equation of our lives. Providing students with their own devices is one step in that important task, and should be supported or encouraged in all schools.

WRITING A THESIS STATEMENT

The thesis, a key organizational tool in any essay, tells readers specifically what you think and what you will say. Without a strong, direct thesis statement, your readers will have to deduce your main idea on their own.

Writing a good thesis sentence really comes down to one thing: simply state your idea and why you think it is true or correct.

Example

Many high schools have begun to adopt 1:1 technology programs, meaning that each school provides every student with a computing device such as a laptop or tablet. Educators who support these initiatives say that the technology allows for more dynamic collaboration and that students need to learn technology skills to compete in the job market. On the other hand, opponents cite increased distraction and the dangers of cyber-bullying or unsupervised internet use as reasons not to provide students with devices.

In your essay, take a position on this question. You may write about either one of the two points of view given, or you may present a different point of view on this question. Use specific reasons and examples to support your position.

Possible thesis statements:

Providing technology to every student is good for schools because it allows students to learn important skills such as typing, web design, or video editing, as well as giving students more opportunities to work together with their classmates and teachers.

I disagree with the idea that schools should provide technology to students because most students will simply be distracted by the free access to games and websites when they should be studying or doing homework.

In a world where technology is improving and changing at a phenomenal rate, schools have a responsibility to teach students how to navigate that technology safely and effectively, and providing each student with a laptop or tablet is one way to help them do that.

PROVIDING SUPPORTING EVIDENCE

Your essay not only needs structured, organized paragraphs, it also needs to provide specific supporting evidence for your argument. Any time you make a general statement, it should be followed by specific evidence that will help to convince the reader that your argument has merit. The specific examples do not give new ideas to the paragraph; rather, they explain or defend the general ideas that have already been stated.

The following are some other examples of general statements and specific statements that provide more detailed support:

GENERAL: Students may get distracted online or access harmful websites.

SPECIFIC: Some students spend too much time using chat features or social media, or they get caught up in online games. Others spend time reading websites that have nothing to do with an assignment.

SPECIFIC: Teens often think they are hidden behind their computer screens. If teenagers give out personal information such as age or location on a website, it can lead to dangerous strangers seeking them out.

GENERAL: Many different types of animals can make good family pets.

SPECIFIC: Labrador Retrievers are friendly and enjoy spending time with the family, though it will be important to walk the dog often.

SPECIFIC: On the other hand, pets such as gerbils, mice, hamsters, or rats can be very affectionate and are much more contained—so it is easier to keep their living area clean.

Example

Below is an example of a paragraph that uses specific supporting ideas in a logical paragraph structure to support the thesis statement in the previous section.

Providing students with their own laptop or tablet will allow them to explore new programs and software in class with teachers and classmates and then practice at home. In schools without laptops for students, classes have to visit computer labs, where they share old, used up computers that often have the keys missing or run so slowly they can barely be turned on before class ends. If a teacher tries to show students how to use a new tool or website, then students have to scramble to follow along and have no chance to explore the possibilities of the new tool. If they have laptops to take home instead, students can do things like practice editing video clips or photographs until they are perfect. They can email a classmate or use shared files to collaborate even after school. If schools expect students to learn these skills, it is their responsibility to provide students enough opportunities to practice them.

This paragraph has some general statements:

… their own laptop or tablet will allow them to explore new programs and software… and then practice…

…it is their responsibility to provide… enough opportunities..

It also has some specific examples to back them up:

…computers… run so slowly they can barely be turned on… students have to scramble to follow along and have no chance to explore…

They can email a classmate or use shared file.s to collaborate…

WRITING WELL

The final considerations for your essay, the polish, if you will, add the touch that will help readers see your argument clearly and understand the complexity and depth of your writing.

Transitions

Transitions are words, sentences, and ideas that help connect one piece of writing to another. You should use them between sentences and between paragraphs. Some common transitions include then, next, in other words, as well, in addition to. Be creative with your transitions, if possible, and make sure you understand what the transition you are using shows about the relationship between the ideas. For instance, the transition although implies that there is some contradiction between the first idea and the second.

Syntax

The way you write sentences is important to maintaining the interest of a reader. Try to begin sentences differently. Make some sentences long and some sentences short. Write simple sentences. Write complex sentences that have complex ideas in them. Readers appreciate variety.

There are four basic types of sentences: simple, compound, complex, and compound-complex. Try to use some of each type. Be careful that the sentences make sense, though—it is better to have clear and simple writing that a reader can understand than to have complex, confusing syntax that does not clearly express the idea.

Word Choice and Tone

The words you choose influence the impression you make on readers. There are two important things you need to do. Firstly, use words that are specific, direct, and appropriate to the task— complex and impressive; simple and direct; or even neutral. Use the best words you know and do your best to avoid using vague, general words such as good, bad, very, or a lot. Words like these have unclear meanings from being used in many different situations —they can mean different things depending on the situation. Secondly, make sure that you actually use words you know! Trying to fit in too many "million-dollar words," may result in using some you do not know as well and thus use incorrectly; try to fit in words that you know make sense in the context.

Editing, Revising, and Proofreading

When writing a timed essay, of course, you should not plan to have very much time for these steps; however, whatever time you have left after drafting should be spent looking over your essay and checking for spelling and grammar mistakes that may interfere with a reader's understanding. Some common mistakes to learn and look out for include subject/verb disagreement; confusing common words like "loose" and "lose;" pronoun/antecedent disagreement; comma splices and run-ons; or fragments.

7

GRAMMAR

Writing essays for the CBEST will require you to understand the basic rules of grammar, punctuation, spelling, and capitalization. The good news is that you have been using these rules since you first began to speak; even if you don't know a lot of the technical terms, many of these rules may be familiar to you.

PARTS OF SPEECH

Nouns and Pronouns

NOUNS are people, places, or things. They are typically the subject of a sentence. For example, in the sentence *The hospital was very clean,* the noun is *hospital;* it is a place. PRONOUNS replace nouns and make sentences sound less repetitive. Take the sentence *Sam stayed home from school because Sam was not feeling well.* The word Sam appears twice in the same sentence. Instead, you can use a pronoun and say *Sam stayed at home because he did not feel well.* Sounds much better, right?

Because pronouns take the place of nouns, they need to agree both in number and gender with the noun they replaced. So, a plural noun needs a plural pronoun, and a feminine noun needs a feminine pronoun. In the previous sentence, for example, the plural pronoun *they* replaced the plural noun pronouns.

SINGULAR PRONOUNS
- I, me, mine, my
- you, your, yours
- he, him, his
- she, her, hers
- it, its

PLURAL PRONOUNS
- we, us, our, ours
- they, them, their, theirs

Examples

Wrong: If a student forgets their homework, it is considered incomplete.

Correct: If a student forgets his or her homework, it is considered incomplete.

Student is a singular noun, but their is a plural pronoun. So, this first sentence is grammatically incorrect. To correct it, replace their with the singular pronoun his or her.

Wrong: Everybody will receive their paychecks promptly.

Correct: Everybody will receive his or her paycheck promptly.

Everybody is a singular noun, but their is a plural pronoun. So, this sentence is grammatically incorrect. To correct it, replace their with the singular pronoun his or her.

Wrong: When a nurse begins work at a hospital, you should wash your hands.

Correct: When a nurse begins work at a hospital, he or she should wash his or her hands.

This sentence begins in third-person perspective and finishes in second-person perspective. So, this sentence is grammatically incorrect. To correct it, ensure the sentence finishes with third-person perspective.

Wrong: After the teacher spoke to the student, she realized her mistake.

Correct: After Mr. White spoke to his student, she realized her mistake. (she and her referring to student)

Correct: After speaking to the student, the teacher realized her own mistake. (her referring to teacher)

This sentence refers to a teacher and a student. But who does she refer to, the teacher or the student? To improve clarity, use specific names or state more specifically who spotted the mistake.

Verbs

Remember the old commercial, "Verb: It's what you do"? That sums up verbs in a nutshell. A verb is the action of a sentence; verbs "do" things. Verb must be conjugated to match the context of the sentence; this can sometimes be tricky because English has many irregular verbs. For example, runs is an action verb in the present tense that becomes ran in the past tense; the linking verb is (which describes a state of being) becomes was in the past tense.

Table 8.1. Conjugations of the verb *to be*

	PAST	PRESENT	FUTURE
SINGULAR	was	is	will be
PLURAL	were	are	will be

As mentioned, verbs must use the correct tense, and that tense must make sense in the context of the sentence. For example, the sentence *I was baking cookies and eat some dough* sounds strange, right? That's because the two verbs *was baking* and *eat* are in different tenses. *Was baking* occurred in the past; *eat*, on the other hand, occurs in the present. Instead, it should be *ate some dough*.

Like pronouns, verbs must agree in number with the noun they refer back to. In the example above, the verb *was* refers back to the singular *I*.

Think of the subject and the verb as sharing a single s. If the noun ends with an s, the noun shouldn't and vice versa.

If the subject is separated from the verb, cross out the phrases between them to make conjugation easier.

If the subject of the sentence was plural, it would need to be modified to read *They were baking cookies and ate some dough.* Note that the verb *ate* does not change form; this is common for verbs in the past tense.

Examples

Wrong: The cat chase the ball while the dogs runs in the yard.

Correct: The cat chases the ball while the dogs run in the yard.

Cat is singular, so it takes a singular verb (which confusingly ends with an s); dogs is plural, so it needs a plural verb.

Wrong: The cars that had been recalled by the manufacturer was returned within a few months.

Correct: The cars that had been recalled by the manufacturer were returned within a few months.

Sometimes, the subject and verb are separated by clauses or phrases. Here, the subject cars is separated from the verb phrase were returned, making it more difficult to conjugate the verb.

Correct: The deer hid in the trees.

Correct: The deer are not all the same size.

The subject of these sentences is a collective noun, which describes a group of people or items. This noun can be singular if its referring to the group as a whole or plural if it refers to each item in the group as a separate entity.

Correct: The doctor and nurse work in the hospital.

Correct: Neither the nurse nor her boss was scheduled to take a vacation.

Correct: Either the patient or her parents need to sign the release forms.

When the subject contains two or more nouns connected by and, that subject is plural and requires a plural verb. Singular subjects joined by or, either/or, neither/nor, or not only/but also remain singular; when these words join plural and singular subjects, the verb should match the closest subject.

Wrong: Because it will rain during the party last night, we had to move the tables inside.

Correct: Because it rained during the party last night, we had to move the tables inside.

All the verb tenses in a sentence need to agree both with each other and with the other information in the sentence. In the first sentence above, the tense doesn't match the other information in the sentence: last night indicates the past (rained) not the future (will rain).

Adjectives and Adverbs

Adjectives are words that describe a noun. Take the sentence *The boy hit the ball*. If you want to know more about the noun *boy*, then you could use an adjective to describe it: *The little boy hit the ball*. An adjective simply provides more information about a noun or subject in a sentence.

For some reason, many people have a difficult time with adverbs, but don't worry! They are really quite simple. Adverbs and adjectives are similar because they provide more information about a part of a sentence; however, they do not describe nouns—that's an adjective's job. Instead, adverbs describe verbs, adjectives, and even other adverbs. For example, in the sentence *The doctor had recently hired a new employee*, the adverb *recently* tells us more about how the action *hired* took place.

Adjectives, adverbs, and modifying phrases (groups of words that together modify another word) should always be placed as close as possible to the word they modify. Separating words from their modifiers can create incorrect or confusing sentences.

Examples

Wrong: Running through the hall, the bell rang and the student knew she was late.

Correct: Running through the hall, the student heard the bell ring and knew she was late.

The phrase running through the hall should be placed next to student, the noun it modifies.

Wrong: Of my two friends, Clara is the most smartest.

Correct: Of my two friends, Clara is more smart.

The first sentence above has two mistakes. First, the word most should only be used when comparing three or more things. Second, the adjective should only be modified with more/most or the suffix -er/-est, not both.

Other Parts of Speech

PREPOSITIONS express the location of a noun or pronoun in relation to other words and phrases in a sentence. For example, in the sentence *The nurse parked her car in a parking garage*, the preposition *in* describes the position of the car in relation to the garage. The noun that follows the preposition is called it's OBJECT. In the example above, the object of the preposition *in* is the noun *parking garage*.

See *Phrases and Clauses* for more on independent and dependent clauses.

CONJUNCTIONS connect words, phrases, and clauses. The conjunctions summarized in the acronym FANBOYS—*for, and, nor, but, or, yet, so*—are called coordinating conjunctions and are used to join independent clauses. For example, in the sentence *The nurse prepared the patient for surgery, and the doctor performed the surgery*, the conjunction *and* joins together the two independent clauses. SUBORDINATING CONJUNCTIONS like *although*, *because*, and *if* join together an independent and dependent clause. In the sentence *She had to ride the subway because her car was broken*, the conjunction *because* joins together the two clauses.

INTERJECTIONS, like *wow* and *hey*, express emotion and are most commonly used in conversation and casual writing.

CONSTRUCTING SENTENCES

Phrases and Clauses

A PHRASE is a group of words acting together that contain either a subject or verb, but not both. Phrases can be made from many different parts of speech. For example, a prepositional phrases includes a preposition and the object of that preposition (e.g., under the table), and a verb phrase includes the main verb and any helping verbs (e.g., had been running). Phrases cannot stand along as a sentence.

A CLAUSE is a group of words that contains both a subject and a verb. There are two types of clauses: independent clauses can stand alone as a sentence, and dependent clauses cannot stand alone. Dependent clauses begin with a subordinating conjunction.

Examples

Classify each of the following as a phrase, independent clause, or dependent clause:

1. I have always wanted to drive a bright red sports car

2. under the bright sky filled with stars

3. because my sister is running late

Number 1 is an independent clause—it has a subject (I) and a verb (have wanted) and has no subordinating conjunction. Number 2 is a phrase made up of a preposition (under), its object (sky), and words that modify sky (bright, filled with stars). Number 3 is a dependent clause—it has a subject (sister), a verb (is running), and a subordinating conjunction (because).

Types of Sentences

A sentence can be classified as simple, compound, complex, or compound-complex based on the type and number of clauses it has.

Table 8.2. Types of Sentences

SENTENCE TYPE	NUMBER OF INDEPENDENT CLAUSES	NUMBER OF DEPENDENT CLAUSES
Simple	1	0
Compound	2+	0
Complex	1	1+
Compound-Complex	2+	1+

A simple sentence consists of only one independent clause. Because there are no dependent clauses in a simple sentence, it can simply be a two-word sentence, with one word being the subject and the other word being the verb (e.g., I ran.). However, a simple sentence can also contain prepositions, adjectives, and adverbs. Even though these additions can extend the length of a simple sentence, it is still considered a simple sentence as long as it doesn't contain any dependent clauses.

Compound sentences have two or more independent clauses and no dependent clauses. Usually a comma and a coordinating conjunction (and, or, but, nor, for, so, and yet) join the independent clauses, though semicolons can be used as well. For example, the sentence My computer broke, so I took it to be repaired is compound.

Complex sentences have one independent clause and at least one dependent clause. In the complex sentence If you lie down with dogs, you'll wake up with fleas, the first clause is dependent (because of the subordinating conjunction if), and the second is independent.

Compound-complex sentences have two or more independent clauses and at least one subordinate clause. For example, the sentence Even though David was a vegetarian, he went with his friends to steakhouses, but he focused on the conversation instead of the food, is compound-complex.

Examples

Classify: San Francisco in the springtime is one of my favorite places to visit.

Although the sentence is lengthy, it is simple because it contains only one subject and verb (San Francisco . . . is) modified by additional phrases.

Classify: I love listening to the radio in the car because I can sing along as loud as I want.

The sentence has one independent clause (I love . . . car) and one dependent (because I . . . want), so it's complex.

Classify: I wanted to get a dog, but I have a fish because my roommate is allergic to pet dander.

This sentence has three clauses: two independent (I wanted . . . dog and I have a fish) and one dependent (because my . . . dander), so it's compound-complex.

Classify: The game was cancelled, but we will still practice on Saturday.

This sentence is made up of two independent clauses joined by a conjunction (but), so it's compound.

CLAUSE PLACEMENT

In addition to the classifications above, sentences can also be defined by the location of the main clause. In a periodic sentence, the main idea of the sentence is held until the end. In a cumulative sentence, the independent clause comes first, and any modifying words or clauses follow it. Note that this type of classification—periodic or cumulative—is not used in place of the simple, compound, complex, or compound-complex classifications. A sentence can be both cumulative and complex, for example.

Examples

Classify: To believe your own thought, to believe that what is true for you in your private heart is true for all men, that is genius.

In this sentence the main independent clause—that is genius—is held until the very end, so it's periodic. It's also simple because it has one independent clause.

Classify: We need the tonic of wildness—to wade sometimes in marshes where the bittern and meadow-hen lurk, and hear the booming of the snipe; to smell the whispering sedge where only some wilder and more solitary fowl builds her nest, and the mink crawls with its belly close to the ground.

Here, the main clause—we need the tonic of wildness—is at the beginning, so the sentence is cumulative. It's also simple because it has one main clause.

Punctuation

The basic rules for using the major punctuation marks are given in the following table.

Table 8.3. How to Use Punctuation

PUNCTUATION	USED FOR	EXAMPLE
Period	ending sentences	Periods go at the end of complete sentences
Question Mark	ending questions	What's the best way to end a sentence?
Exclamation Point	ending sentences that show extreme emotion	I'll never understand how to use commas!
Comma	joining two independent clauses (always with a coordinating conjunction)	Commas can be used to join clauses, but they must always be followed by a coordinating conjunction
	setting apart introductory and nonessential words and phrases	Commas, when used properly, set apart extra information in a sentence.
	separating items in a list	My favorite punctuation marks include the colon, semicolon, and period.

Semicolon	joining together two independent clauses (never with a conjunction)	I love exclamation points; they make sentences so exciting!
Colon	introducing a list, explanation or definition	When I see a colon, I know what to expect: more information.
Apostrophe	form contractions	It's amazing how many people can't use apostrophes correctly.
	show possession	Parentheses are my sister's favorite punctuation; she finds commas' rules confusing.
Quotation Marks	indicate a direct quote	I said to her, "Tell me more about parentheses."

Examples

Wrong: Her roommate asked her to pick up milk, and watermelon from the grocery store.

Correct: Her roommate asked her to pick up milk and watermelon from the grocery store.

Commas are only needed when joining three items in a series; this sentence only has two (milk and watermelon).

Wrong: The coach of the softball team—who had been in the job for only a year, quit unexpectedly on Friday.

Correct: The coach of the softball team—who had been in the job for only a year—quit unexpectedly on Friday.

Correct: The coach of the softball team, who had been in the job for only a year, quit unexpectedly on Friday.

When setting apart nonessential words and phrases, you can use either dashes or commas, but not both.

Wrong: I'd like to order a hamburger, from my favorite restaurant, but my friend says I should get a sandwich instead.

Correct: I'd like to order a hamburger from my favorite restaurant, but my friend says I should get a sandwich instead.

Prepositional phrases are almost always essential to the sentences, meaning they don't need to be set apart with commas. Note that the second comma remains because it is separating two independent clauses.

CAPITALIZATION

- The first word of a sentence is always capitalized.
- The first letter of a proper nouns is always capitalized. (We're going to Chicago on Wednesday.)
- The first letter of an adjectives derived from a proper noun is capitalized. (The play was described by critics as Shakespearian.)

- Titles are capitalized if they precede the name they modify. (President Obama met with Joe Biden, his vice president.)
- Months are capitalized, but not the names of the seasons. (Snow fell in March even though winter was over.)
- School subjects are not capitalized unless they are themselves proper nouns. (I will have chemistry and French tests tomorrow.)

Example

Which sentence contains an error in capitalization?

A) She wrote many angry letters, but only senator Phillips responded to her request.

B) Matthew lives on Main Street and takes the bus to work every weekday.

C) Maria's goal has always wanted to be an astronaut, so she's studying astronomy in school.

D) Although his birthday is in February, Will decided to celebrate early by eating at Francisco's, his favorite restaurant.

Sentence A) contains an error: the title senator should be capitalized when it's used in front of a name.

TRANSITIONS

Transitions join together two ideas and also explain the logical relationship between those ideas. For example, the transition *because* tells you that two things have a cause and effect relationship, while the transitional phrase *on the other hand* introduces a contradictory idea. On the CBEST Writing section, you will definitely need to make good use of transitions in your essay.

Table 8.4. Common Transition Words

CAUSE AND EFFECT	as a result, because, consequently, due to, if/then, so, therefore, thus
SIMILARITY	also, likewise, similarly
CONTRAST	but, however, in contrast, on the other hand, nevertheless, on the contrary, yet
CONCLUDING	briefly, finally, in conclusion, in summary, thus, to, conclude
ADDITION	additionally, also, as well, further, furthermore, in addition, moreover
EXAMPLES	in other words, for example, for instance, to illustrate
TIME	after, before, currently, later, recently, since, subsequently, then, while

CONTINUE

Examples

Choose the transition that would best fit in the blank.

1. Clara's car breaks down frequently. _____, she decided to buy a new one.

2. Chad scored more points than any other player on his team. _____, he is often late to practice, so his coach won't let him play in the game Saturday.

3. Miguel will often his lunch outside. _____, on Wednesday he took his sandwich to the park across from his office.

4. Alex set the table _____ the lasagna finished baking in the oven.

A) however

B) for example

C) while

D) therefore

Sentence 1 is describing a cause (her car breaks down) and an effect (she'll buy a new one), so the correct transition is therefore. Sentence 2 includes a contrast: it would make sense for Chad to play in the game, but he isn't, so the best transition is however. In Sentence 3, the clause after the transition is an example, so the best transition is for example. In Sentence 4, two things are occurring at the same time, so the best transition is while.

PART IV: TEST YOUR KNOWLEDGE

8

PRACTICE TEST: READING

Read the passage below; then answer the six questions that follow.

Skin coloration and markings have an important role to play in the world of snakes. Those intricate diamonds, stripes, and swirls help animals hide from predators and advertise to mates. Perhaps most importantly (for us humans, anyway), the markings can also indicate whether the snake is venomous. While it might seem counterintuitive for a poisonous snake to stand out in bright red or blue, that fancy costume tells any approaching predator that eating him would be a bad idea.

If you see a flashy looking snake out the woods, though, those marking don't necessarily mean it's poisonous: some snakes have a found a way to ward off predators without the actual venom. The California Kingsnake, for example, has very similar markings to the venomous Coral snake with whom it frequently shares a habitat. However, the Kingsnake is actually nonvenomous; it's merely pretending to be dangerous to eat. The Kingsnake itself eats lizards, rodents, birds, and even other snakes. A predatory hawk or eagle, usually hunting from high in the sky, can't tell the difference between the two species, and so the Kingsnake gets passed over and lives another day.

1. The writer's main purpose in the passage is to:

    A) explain how the markings on a snake are related to whether it is venomous.

    B) teach readers the difference between Coral snakes and Kingsnakes.

    C) illustrate why snakes are dangerous.

    D) demonstrate how animals survive in difficult environments.

    E) explain what Kingsnakes eat.

2. Based on information contained in the passage, it is reasonable to infer that

    A) The Kingsnake is dangerous to humans.

    B) The Coral snake and the Kingsnake are both hunted by the same predators.

    C) It's safe to handle snakes in the woods because you can easily tell whether they're poisonous.

    D) The Kingsnake changes its marking when hawks or eagles are close by.

    E) Coral snakes and Kingsnakes eat the same prey.

3. Which of the following statements best expresses the central idea of the passage?

A) Humans can use coloration and markings on snakes to determine whether they're poisonous.

B) Animals often use coloration and markings to attract mates and warn predators that they're poisonous.

C) The California Kingsnake and Coral snake have nearly identical markings.

D) Venomous snakes often have bright markings, although nonvenomous snakes can also mimic those colors.

E) Predators don't hunt Coral snakes or Kingsnakes because they can't tell whether the snakes are venomous.

4. Which sentence is least relevant to the main idea of the main idea of the passage?

A) Perhaps most importantly (for us humans, anyway), the markings can also indicate whether the snake is venomous.

B) The California Kingsnake, for example, has very similar markings to the venomous Coral snake with whom it frequently shares a habitat.

C) However, the Kingsnake is actually nonvenomous; it's merely pretending to be dangerous to eat.

D) Skin coloration and markings have an important role to play in the world of snakes.

E) The Kingsnake itself eats lizards, rodents, birds, and even other snakes.

5. Which of the following is the best meaning of the word *intricate* as it is used in the first paragraph of the passage?

A) natural

B) colorful

C) purposeful

D) changeable

E) complicated

6. According to the passage, what is the difference between Kingsnakes and Coral snakes?

A) Both Kingsnakes and Coral snakes are nonvenomous, but Coral snakes have colorful markings.

B) Both Kingsnakes and Coral snakes are venomous, but Kingsnakes have colorful markings.

C) Kingsnakes are nonvenomous while Coral snakes are venomous.

D) Coral snakes are nonvenomous while Kingsnakes are venomous.

E) Both Kingsnakes and Coral snakes are venomous and have colorful markings.

Read the passage below; then answer the six questions that follow.

Hand washing is one of our simplest and most powerful weapons against infection. The idea behind hand washing is deceptively simple. Many illnesses are spread when people touch infected surfaces, such as door handles or other people's hands, and then touch their own eyes, mouths, or noses. So, if pathogens can be removed from the hands before they spread, infections can be prevented. When done correctly, hand washing can prevent the spread of many dangerous bacteria and viruses, including those that cause the flu, the common cold, diarrhea, and many acute respiratory illnesses.

The most basic method of hand washing involves only soap and water. Just twenty seconds of scrubbing with soap and a complete rinsing with water is enough to kill and/or wash away many pathogens. The process doesn't even require warm water—studies have shown that cold water is just as effective at reducing the number of microbes on the hands. Antibacterial soaps are also available, although several studies have shown that simple soap and cold water is just as effective.

In recent years, hand sanitizers have become popular as an alternative to hand washing. These gels, liquids, and foams contain a high concentration of alcohol (usually at least 60 percent) which kills most bacteria and fungi; they can also be effective against some, but not all, viruses. There is a downside to hand sanitizer, however. Because the sanitizer isn't rinsed from hands, it only kills pathogens and does nothing to remove organic matter. So, hands "cleaned" with hand sanitizer may still harbor pathogens. Thus, while hand sanitizer can be helpful in situations where soap and clean water isn't available, a simple hand washing is still the best option.

7. Which of the following is the best meaning of the word *harbor* as it is used in the last paragraph of the passage?

   A) to disguise

   B) to hide

   C) to wash away

   D) to give a home

   E) to destroy

8. Which of the following best organizes the main topics addressed in this passage?

   A) I. Comparison of hand washing methods
      II. The disadvantages of hand sanitizer

   B) I. The importance of hand washing in preventing disease
      II. The benefits and problems with various methods of hand washing

   C) I. The relationship between hand washing and disease prevention
      II. Comparison of regular and anti-bacterial soaps

   D) I. How to effectively wash hands using soap and water
      II. How to clean hands using hand sanitizer

   E) I. Methods of disease transmission
      II. Effectiveness of anti-bacterial soaps

9. Which sentence, if inserted into the blank line in the sentence below, would be most consistent with the pattern of logic developed in the passage?

   Knowing that the temperature of the water does not affect the effectiveness of hand washing, it can be concluded that water plays an important role in hand washing because it

   _____

   A) has antibacterial properties

   B) physically removes pathogens from hands

   C) cools hands to make them inhospitable for dangerous bacteria

   D) is hot enough to kill bacteria

   E) contains at least 60 percent alcohol

10. The writer's main purpose in the passage is to:

   A) persuade readers of the importance and effectiveness of hand washing with soap and cold water.

   B) dissuade readers from using hand sanitizer.

   C) explain how many common diseases are spread.

   D) describe the health benefits provided by hand washing and hand sanitizer.

11. Information presented in the passage best supports which of the following conclusions?

   A) Hand washing would do little to limit infections that spread through particles in the air.

   B) Hand washing is not necessary for people who do not touch their eyes, mouths, or noses with their hands.

   C) Hand sanitizer serves no purpose and should not be used as an alternative to hand washing.

   D) Hand sanitizer will likely soon replace hand washing as the preferred method of removing pathogens from hands.

   E) Hand sanitizer with an alcohol percentage below 60 percent will be as effective as hand washing.

12. Which of the following is not a fact stated in the passage?

   A) Many infections occur because people get pathogens on their hands and then touch their own eyes, mouths, or noses.

   B) Cold water is just as effective at removing pathogens as warm water.

   C) Most hand sanitizers have a concentration of at least 60 percent alcohol.

   D) Hand sanitizer can be an acceptable alternative to hand washing when soap and water aren't available.

   E) Antibacterial soaps and warm water are the best way to remove pathogens from hands.

CONTINUE →

Read the passage below; then answer the five questions that follow.

It could be said that the great battle between the North and South we call the Civil War was a battle for individual identity. The states of the South had their own culture, one based on farming, independence, and the rights of both man and state to determine their own paths. Similarly, the North had forged its own identity as a center of centralized commerce and manufacturing. This clash of lifestyles was bound to create tension, and this tension was bound to lead to war. But people who try to sell you this narrative are wrong. The Civil War was a not a battle of cultural identities—it was a battle about slavery. All other explanations for the war are either a direct consequence of the South's desire for wealth at the expense of her fellow man or a fanciful invention to cover up this sad portion of our nation's history. And it cannot be denied that this time in our past was very sad indeed. By denying our history, we make it even sadder.

13. The writer's main purpose in the passage is to:

   A) convince readers that slavery was the main cause of the Civil War.

   B) illustrate the cultural differences between the North and the South before the Civil War

   C) persuade readers that the North deserved to win the Civil War

   D) demonstrate that the history of the Civil War is too complicated to be understood clearly

   E) present a balanced argument about the causes of the Civil War

14. Which of the following statements best expresses the central idea of the passage?

   A) The Civil War was the result of cultural differences between the North and South.

   B) The Civil War was caused by the South's reliance on slave labor.

   C) The North's use of commerce and manufacturing allowed it to win the war.

   D) The South's belief in the rights of man and state cost them the war.

   E) Historian should accept that the Civil War was a shameful period in our nation's history.

15. Which of the following sentences from the passage best expresses a fact rather than an opinion?

   A) By denying our history, we make it even sadder.

   B) The states of the South had their own culture, one based on farming, independence, and the rights of both man and state to determine their own paths.

   C) The Civil War was a not a battle of cultural identities—it was a battle about slavery.

   D) And it cannot be denied that this time in our past is very sad indeed.

   E) But people who try to sell you this narrative are wrong.

16. Which of the following indicates how the author would likely state his position on the Civil War?

   A) The Civil War was the result of cultural differences between the North and South.

   B) The Civil War was caused by the South's reliance on slave labor.

   C) The North's use of commerce and manufacturing allowed it to win the war.

   D) The South's belief in the rights of man and state cost them the war.

   E) Historians do not understand what caused the Civil War.

17. Which of the following is the best meaning of the word *fanciful* as it is used in the passage?

   A) complicated

   B) imaginative

   C) successful

   D) unfortunate

   E) gilded

Read the passage below; then answer the two questions that follow.

Mason was one of those guys who just always seemed at home. Stick him on bus, and he'd make three new friends; when he joined a team, it was only a matter of time before he was elected captain. This particular skill rested almost entirely in his eyes. These brown orbs seemed lit from within, and when Mason focused that fire, it was impossible not to feel its warmth. People sought out Mason for the feeling of comfort he so easily created, and anyone with a good joke would want to tell it to Mason. His laughter started with a spark in his eyes that traveled down to create his wide, open smile.

18. Based on information contained in the passage, it is reasonable to infer that

   A) Mason wishes people would tell him more jokes.

   B) Mason is very good at sports.

   C) Mason does not like when strangers approach him.

   D) Mason does not laugh often.

   E) Mason has many friends.

19. Which of the following statements best expresses the central idea of the passage?

   A) Mason was one of those guys who just always seemed at home.

   B) Stick him on bus, and he'd make three new friends; when he joined a team, it was only a matter of time before he was elected captain.

   C) These brown orbs seemed lit from within, and when Mason focused that fire, it was impossible not to feel its warmth.

   D) People sought out Mason for the feeling of comfort he so easily created, and anyone with a good joke would want to tell it to Mason.

   E) His laughter started with a spark in his eyes that traveled down to create his wide, open smile

Use the pie chart below to answer the question that follows.

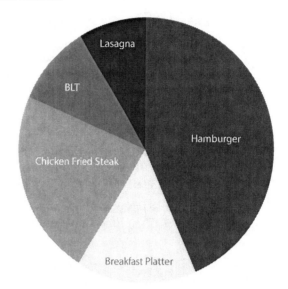

Figure 10.1 Daily Food Order at Gigi's Diner

20. Which item do customers order the most of at Gigi's Diner?

   A) Lasagna

   B) BLT

   C) Hamburgers

   D) Breakfast platters

   E) Chicken fried steak

Use the table of contents below to answer the question that follows.

CONTINUE

21. Which of the following lists includes only subheadings?

A) Plymouth, Jamestown, British Victories, and A New Century

B) American Victories, British Victories, A New Century, and The Ratification Years

C) American Victories, British Victories, The Constitutional Convention, and The Ratification Years

D) Early Settlement, The American Revolution, A New Century, and The Ratification Years

E) Plymouth, Jamestown, The American Revolution, The Ratification Years

Use the table of contents below from a travel book to answer the question that follows.

> **Chapter 3: Planning Your Vacation**
> 1. Getting There
>   A. Air Travel
>   B. Traveling by Train
>   C. _____
>   D. Taking the Bus
> 2. Accommodations
> 3. Dining

22. Based on the pattern in the table of contents above, which of the following is a reasonable heading to insert in the blank spot?

A) Choosing a Destination

B) Navigating the Airport

C) Finding a Hotel

D) Road Trips

E) Budgets

Use the table of contents below to answer the two questions that follow.

> **Advanced Mathematics**
> 1. Pre-Calculus, p. 137 - 225
>   A. Quadratic Equations, p. 137 - 178
>   B. Trigonometry, p. 179 - 225
> 2. Calculus, p. 226 - 314
>   A. Limits, p. 226-240
>   B. Derivatives, p. 241-289
>   C. Integrals, p. 290-314
> 3. Differential Equations, p. 315-452

23. Which of the following topic would be covered on page 237?

A) Quadratic Equations

B) Integrals

C) Trigonometry

D) Differential Equations

E) Limits

24. On which of the following pages would you find information on integrals?

A) 145

B) 215

C) 275

D) 302

E) 412

Read the passage below; then answer the six questions that follow.

Taking a person's temperature is one of the most basic and common health care tasks. Everyone from nurses to emergency medical technicians to concerned parents has needed to grab a thermometer and take somebody's temperature. But what's the best way to get an accurate reading? The answer depends on the situation.

The most common way people measure body temperature is orally. A simple digital or disposable thermometer is placed under the tongue for a few minutes, and the task is done. There are many situations, however, when measuring temperature orally isn't an option. For example, when a person can't breathe through his nose, he won't be able to keep his mouths closed long enough to get an accurate reading. In these situations, it's often preferable to place the thermometer in the rectum or armpit. Using the rectum also has the added benefit of providing a much more accurate reading than other locations can provide.

It's also often the case that certain people, like agitated patients or fussy babies, won't be able to sit still long enough for an accurate reading. In this situations, it's best to use a thermometer that works much more quickly, such as one that measures temperature in the ear or at the temporal artery. No matter which method is chosen, however, it's important to check the average temperature for the chosen region, as these can vary by several degrees.

25. The writer's main purpose in the passage is to:

A) advocate for the use of thermometers that measure temperature in the ear or at the temporal artery.

B) explain the methods available to measure a person's temperature and the situation where each method is appropriate.

C) warn readers that the average temperature of the human body varies by region.

D) discuss how nurses use different types of thermometers depending on the type of patient they are examining.

E) persuade parents to purchase several different types of thermometers.

26. Which of the following statements best expresses the central idea of the passage?

A) It's important that everyone know the best way to take a person's temperature in any given situation.

B) The most common method of taking a person's temperature—orally—isn't appropriate is some situations.

C) The most accurate way to take a temperature is placing a digital thermometer in the rectum.

D) There are many different ways to take a person's temperature, and which is appropriate will depend on the situation.

E) Nurses, parents, and emergency medical technicians all need to be aware of the many types of thermometers available.

27. Which of the following is the best meaning of the word *agitated* as it is used in the last paragraph of the passage?

A) obviously upset

B) quickly moving

C) violently ill

D) slightly dirty

E) quietly confused

28. According to the passage, why is it sometimes preferable to take a person's temperature rectally?

A) Rectal readings are more accurate than oral readings.

B) Many people cannot sit still long enough to have their temperatures taken orally.

C) Temperature readings can vary widely between regions of the body.

D) Many people do not have access to quick-acting thermometers.

E) Babies have trouble holding a thermometer under their tongues.

29. Which of the following assumptions most influenced the writer's argument in the passage?

A) Most people will have access to only one type of thermometer at home.

B) Nurses take patients' temperature more often than doctors.

C) Oral thermometers are the most commonly available and easy to use thermometer.

D) People who do not work in health care do not need to take temperatures often.

E) Getting an accurate temperature reading is an important part of basic medical care.

CONTINUE →

30. Which statement is not a fact from the passage?

   A) Taking a temperature in the ear or at the temporal artery is more accurate than taking it orally.

   B) If an individual cannot breathe through his nose, taking his temperature orally will likely give an inaccurate reading.

   C) The standard human body temperature varies depending on whether it's measured in the mouth, rectum, armpit, ear, or temporal artery.

   D) The most common way to measure temperature is by placing a thermometer in the mouth.

   E) Thermometers that measure temperature in the ear or at the temporal artery work faster than oral thermometers.

Read the passage below; then answer the five questions that follow.

The Jazz Age

In recent decades, jazz has been associated with New Orleans and festivals like Mardi Gras, but in the 1920s jazz was a booming trend whose influence reached into many aspects of American culture. In fact, the years between World War I and the Great Depression were known as the Jazz Age, a term coined by F. Scott Fitzgerald in his famous novel *The Great Gatsby*. Sometimes also called the Roaring Twenties, this time period saw major urban cities experiencing new economic, cultural, and artistic vitality. In the United States, musicians flocked to cities like New York and Chicago, which would became famous hubs for jazz musicians. Ella Fitzgerald, for example, moved from Virginia to New York City to begin her much lauded singing career, and jazz pioneer Louis Armstrong got his big break in Chicago.

Jazz music was played by and for a more expressive and freed populace than the United States had previously seen. Women gained the right to vote and were openly seen drinking and dancing to jazz music. This period marked the emergence of the flapper, a woman determined to make a statement about her new role in society. Jazz music also provided the soundtrack for the explosion of African American art and culture now known as the Harlem Renaissance. In addition to Fitzgerald and Armstrong, numerous musicians, including Duke Ellington, Fats Waller, and Bessie Smith, promoted

their distinctive and complex music as an integral part of the emerging African American culture.

31. Which of the following best organizes the main topics addressed in this passage?

   A) I. The influence of jazz music on women and African Americans

      II. Prominent jazz musicians

   B) I. The impact of F. Scott Fitzgerald on the Jazz Age

      II. The role jazz music played in the women's right-to-vote movement

   C) I. Misconceptions about jazz music

      II. The role of jazz music in the Harlem Renaissance

   D) I. The importance of big cities in the growth of jazz music

      II. The role jazz music played in the lives on minorities during the 1920s

   E) I. The cultural importance of the Jazz Age

      II. How jazz music shaped the experiences of minority groups

32. Information presented in the passage best supports which of the following conclusions?

   A) Jazz music was important to minority groups struggling for social equality in the 1920s.

   B) Duke Ellington, Fats Waller, and Bessie Smith were the most important jazz musicians of the Harlem Renaissance.

   C) Women were able to gain the right to vote with the help of jazz musicians.

   D) Duke Ellington, Fats Waller, and Bessie Smith all supported women's right to vote.

   E) The Jazz Age was a period during which African American musicians struggled to be heard.

33. Which of the following inferences may be drawn from information presented in the passage?
    A)   F. Scott Fitzgerald supported jazz musicians in New York and Chicago.
    B)   Jazz music is no longer as popular as it once was.
    C)   Both women and African Americans used jazz music as a way of expressing their newfound freedom.
    D)   Flapper and African American musicians worked together to produce jazz music.
    E)   People who played jazz music in the 1920s would be disappointed with festivals like Mardi Gras.

34. The writer's main purpose in the passage is to:
    A)   explain the role jazz musicians played in the Harlem Renaissance
    B)   inform the reader about the many important musicians playing jazz in the 1920s
    C)   discuss how jazz influenced important cultural movements in the 1920s
    D)   provide a history of jazz music in the 20th century
    E)   explain how New Orleans became the center of the jazz culture

Read the passage below; then answer the five questions that follow.

The bacteria, fungi, insects, plants, and animals that live together in a habitat have evolved to share a pool of limited resources. They've competed for water, minerals, nutrients, sunlight, and space, sometimes for thousands or even millions of years. As these communities have evolved, the species in them have developed complex, long-term interspecies interactions known as symbiotic relationships.

Ecologists characterize these interactions based on whether each party benefits. In mutualism both individuals benefit, while in synnecrosis both organisms are harmed. A relationship where one individual benefits and the other is harmed is known as parasitism. Examples of these relationships can easily be seen in any ecosystem. Pollination, for example, is mutualistic—pollinators get nutrients from the flower, and the plant is able to reproduce—while tapeworms, which steal nutrients from their host, are parasitic.

There's yet another class of symbiosis that is controversial among scientists. As it's long been defined, commensalism is a relationship where one species benefits and the other is unaffected. But is it possible for two species to interact and for one to remain completely unaffected? Often, relationships described as commensal include one species that feeds on another species' leftovers; remoras, for instance, will attach themselves to sharks and eat the food particles they leave behind. It might seem like the shark gets nothing from the relationship, but a closer look will show that sharks in fact benefit from remoras, which clean the sharks' skin and remove parasites. In fact, many scientists claim that relationships currently described as consensual are just mutualistic or parasitic in ways that haven't been discovered yet. Given the forces of natural selection that shape these relationships, it seems likely that they'll be proven right one day.

35. The writer's main purpose in the passage is to:
    A)   argue that commensalism isn't actually found in nature.
    B)   describe the many types of symbiotic relationships.
    C)   explain how competition for resources results in long-term interspecies relationships.
    D)   provide examples of the many different types of interspecies interactions.
    E)   compare the many different inter-species relationships found in nature.

36. Which of the following is the best meaning of the word *controversial* as it is used in the second paragraph of the passage?
    A)   ignored
    B)   hated
    C)   confused
    D)   debated
    E)   forgotten

→

CONTINUE

37. Why is commensalism controversial among scientists?

   A) Many scientists believe that an interspecies interaction where one species is unaffected does not exist.

   B) Some scientists believe that relationships where one species feeds on the leftovers of another should be classified as parasitism.

   C) Because remoras and sharks have a mutualistic relationship, no interactions should be classified as commensalism.

   D) Only relationships among animal species should be classified as commensalism.

   E) Commensalism has already been proven not to exist in nature.

38. Based on information contained in the passage, it is reasonable to infer what about symbiotic relationships?

   A) Scientists cannot decide how to classify symbiotic relationships among species.

   B) The majority of interspecies interactions are parasitic because most species do not get along.

   C) If two species are involved in a parasitic relationship, one of the species will eventually become extinct.

   D) Symbiotic relationships evolve as the species that live in a community adapt to their environments and each other.

   E) Most interspecies interactions are mutualistic because these relationships help individuals survive.

39. Which of the following sentences in the passage best expresses an opinion rather than a fact?

   A) Ecologists characterize these interactions based on whether each party benefits.

   B) A relationship where one individual benefits and the other is harmed is known as parasitism.

   C) There's yet another class of symbiosis that is controversial among scientists.

   D) In fact, many scientists claim that relationships currently described as consensual are just mutualistic or parasitic in ways that haven't been discovered yet.

   E) Given the forces of natural selection that shape these relationships, it seems likely that they'll be proven right one day.

Read the passage below; then answer the three questions that follow.

Whenever Vi entered that old house, it felt like she was coming home. _____ she hadn't lived there in almost twenty years, the memories of the years she had spent there felt as fresh as the newly fallen snow that blanketed the yard. When she walked through the living room she didn't see the rickety old chairs and peeling paint—she saw the many evenings she'd enjoyed there with her mom, dad, and kid sister. To her, the old dining room didn't smell like dust and moldy table linens; it smelled like home-cooked meals.

Vi's sister, _____ , worried about the more practical matters. That dust and mold had been accumulating in the house ever since their mother moved out, and it didn't seem like their father planned to do anything about it. She hired cleaners, plumbers, and painters, but her father just sent them away.

40. Which words or phrases, if inserted in order into the blanks in the passage, would help the reader understand the sequence of the writer's ideas?

   A) Because; however

   B) Although; similarly

   C) Meanwhile; consequently

   D) In fact; as a result

   E) Even though; on the other hand

41. Based on information contained in the passage, it is reasonable to infer that

A) Vi and her sister had an unhappy childhood.

B) Vi and her sister are going to force their father to sell his house.

C) Vi and her sister disagree about how to help their father.

D) Vi and her sister don't ever talk to their mother.

E) Vi and her sister will hire cleaners to help their father.

42. Which of the following would be the most appropriate title for this passage?

A) Vi and Her Father

B) A Daughter's Fond Memories

C) How to Keep a House Clean

D) A Disagreement Between Sisters

E) A Father's Loss

Use the table of contents below to answer the question that follows.

43. According to the index above, where might the reader find information about truthfulness?

A) 229

B) 231

C) 234

D) 237

E) 241

Use the table of contents below to answer the question that follows.

44. Which of the following headings is out of place?

A) The Stories Behind Famous Paintings

B) Notable Sculpting Techniques

C) Recipes for Common Dishes

D) Textiles and Tapestries

E) Popular Instruments and Lyrics

Use the table of contents below to answer the question that follows.

45. Examine the headings above. Based on the pattern, which of the following is a reasonable heading to insert in the blank spot?

A) Weatherproofing the Patio

B) Adding Insulation in the Attic

C) Choosing a New Dishwasher

D) Updating Plumbing and Fixtures

E) Landscaping with Native Plants

→
CONTINUE

Use the pie chart below to answer the question that follows.

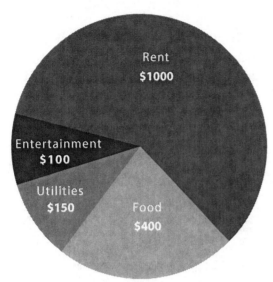

Figure 10.2. Monthly Expense

46. According to the graph above, what accounts for the largest expense per month?

    A) Entertainment

    B) Utilities

    C) Food

    D) Rent

    E) Insurance

Use the table of contents below to answer the question that follows.

47. According to the index above, which of the following pages would include information on weight loss?

    A) 62

    B) 75

    C) 87

    D) 98

    E) 103

Read the passage below; then answer the three questions that follow.

There's no denying the cuteness of a puppy—those big eyes and boundless energy can bring joy to even the sourest of days. It's that sense of joy that brings so many future pet owners to pet stores and dog breeders to pick out their newest family members.

_____ puppies don't stay puppies forever. In just a few short years, that little bouncing bundle of fur will grow into a full-size dog, and, unfortunately, many families just aren't ready to handle that responsibility. _____ , every year tens of thousands of dogs end up in shelters once they reach adulthood. Perhaps the dog grew larger than the owners expected, or the owners weren't able to provide the training that turns a puppy into a well-behaved adult. Whatever the reason, animal rescue shelters are overrun with adult dogs that need good homes.

48. The writer's argument in the passage is mainly addressed to:

    A) families with dogs

    B) dog shelter workers

    C) dog trainers

    D) pet store workers

    E) people adopting dogs

49. Which of the following assumptions most influenced the writer's argument in the passage?

    A) People have a responsibility to provide safe, nurturing homes to all dogs.

    B) Pet store owners usually act in the best interest of the dogs.

    C) Pet shelters have adequate resources to care for large number of homeless adult dogs.

    D) Once families adopt a dog, they might choose to surrender the dog to a shelter.

    E) Adult dogs can often be easier to care for than puppies.

50. Which words or phrases, if inserted **in order** into the blank lines in the passage, would help the reader understand the sequence of the writer's ideas?

A) However; On the other hand

B) Further; Therefore

C) For example; In contrast

D) Yet; More importantly

E) But; Consequently

Practice Test: Reading Answer Key

1.	A)		26.	D)
2.	B)		27.	A)
3.	D)		28.	A)
4.	E)		29.	E)
5.	E)		30.	A)
6.	C)		31.	E)
7.	D)		32.	A)
8.	B)		33.	C)
9.	B)		34.	C)
10.	D)		35.	B)
11.	A)		36.	D)
12.	E)		37.	A)
13.	A)		38.	D)
14.	B)		39.	E)
15.	B)		40.	E)
16.	B)		41.	C)
17.	B)		42.	D)
18.	E)		43.	C)
19.	A)		44.	C)
20.	C)		45.	D)
21.	C)		46.	D)
22.	D)		47.	B)
23.	E)		48.	E)
24.	D)		49.	A)
25.	B)		50.	E)

PRACTICE TEST: MATHEMATICS

1. Alex can pack 8 boxes of food every 90 minutes. How many boxes of food can be packed in 6 hours?

    A)   5

    B)   16

    C)   24

    D)   30

    E)   48

2. A dry cleaner charges $3 per shirt, $6 per pair of pants, and an extra $5 per item for mending. Annie drops off 5 shirts and 4 pairs of pants, 2 of which needed mending. Assuming the cleaner charges an 8% sales tax, what will be Annie's total bill?

    A) $45.08

    B) $49.00

    C) $52.92

    D) $56.16

    E) $88.20

3. If the area of a square quilt is 16 square feet, how many feet is the quilt's perimeter?

    A)   8 feet

    B)   12 feet

    C)   16 feet

    D)   24 feet

    E)   32 feet

4. Which of the following mathematical statements is correct?

    A) $4\frac{4}{5} > 4\frac{2}{5} > 3\frac{4}{5}$

    B) $3\frac{4}{5} > 4\frac{2}{5} > 4\frac{4}{5}$

    C) $4\frac{2}{5} > 4\frac{4}{5} > 3\frac{4}{5}$

    D) $4\frac{4}{5} > 3\frac{4}{5} > 4\frac{2}{5}$

    E) $3\frac{4}{5} > 4\frac{4}{5} > 4\frac{2}{5}$

5. Molly wants to make a headband using 1 of 5 pieces of ribbon. The ribbon must go around her 22 inch head and have between 4 and 6 inches of extra ribbon for her to tie into a knot. Which of the following pieces of ribbon will work best?

    A) $1\frac{1}{2}$ feet

    B)   2 feet

    C) $2\frac{1}{3}$ feet

    D) $2\frac{3}{4}$ feet

    E) $2\frac{5}{8}$ feet

6. Nick needs to purchase a study guide for a test. The study guide costs $80.00, and the sales tax is 8.25%. Nick has $100. How much change will Nick receive back?

    A) $0.00

    B) $4.75

    C) $6.20

    D) $7.45

    E) $13.40

7. The expression $162 + 3 \times (-10) \div 2$ simplifies to which of the following?

    A) −825

    B) −121

    C) 66

    D) 147

    E) 825

8. Which of the following numbers is between 3,125,700 and 3,438,200?

    A) 3,117,320

    B) 3,125,850

    C) 3,472,500

    D) 3,495,340

    E) 3,652,170

9. Jun and Allison need to make 72 sandwiches for their local food bank. Jun has made 23 sandwiches and Allison has made 6 sandwiches. How many more do they need to make?

    A) 37

    B) 43

    C) 49

    D) 54

    E) 66

10. A shirt originally priced at $40 is on sale for $30. What percent has the shirt been discounted?

    A) 10%

    B) 25%

    C) 33%

    D) 70%

    E) 75%

11. Leslie needs to make a pie and some cupcakes. She uses half of her butter to make the pie, and then uses a quarter of the remaining butter to make the cupcakes. If she has 2 cups of butter left, how much did she have before she made the pie?

    A) 4 cups

    B) 6 cups

    C) 6.5 cups

    D) 8 cups

    E) 8.5 cups

12. Tiling costs $2.89 per square foot. What would be the cost to tile a kitchen that is 4 yards long and 5 yards wide?

    A) $26.01

    B) $57.80

    C) $520.20

    D) $570.80

    E) $730.40

13. The average distance from the Earth to the moon is 238,857 miles. At the point in the moon's orbit when it's closest to the Earth, the moon is 27,086 miles closer. Which of the following is the best estimate of the distance between the Earth and moon when they are closest?

    A) 211,000

    B) 212,000

    C) 213,000

    D) 265,000

    E) 266,000

14. Which of the following is the best estimate for $15,886 \times 210$?

    A) 33,000,000

    B) 7,600,000

    C) 3,300,000

    D) 76,000

    E) 33,000

15. Solve for x.

    $7(x - 6) + 21 = 0$

    A) −6

    B) −3

    C) 0

    D) 2

    E) 3

16. The local parks department is planting trees. They have 6 packs of seedlings that contain 12 trees each. If they're going to plant trees in 4 parks, how many trees will go in each park?

    A)   4 trees

    B)   8 trees

    C)   12 trees

    D)   18 trees

    E)   24 trees

17. Use the mathematical statement below to answer the question that follows.

    $\frac{3}{8} < \underline{\quad} < \frac{9}{16}$

    Which of the following values when entered in the box will satisfy the statement above?

    A) $\frac{1}{4}$

    B) $\frac{1}{2}$

    C) $\frac{5}{8}$

    D) $\frac{3}{4}$

    E) $\frac{15}{16}$

18. A store sold 70 hammers in a week. If they sold 35% of their stock, how many hammers did they have at the beginning of the week?

    A)   100

    B)   110

    C)   140

    D)   150

    E)   200

19. John is 5 feet 11 inches tall, and Peter is 6 feet 5 inches tall. How much taller is Peter than John?

    A)   6 inches

    B)   7 inches

    C)   1 foot

    D)   1 foot 6 inches

    E)   1 foot 7 inches

20. If $\frac{1}{3}$ of a 12-inch ruler is broken off, how much is left behind?

    A)   3 inches

    B)   4 inches

    C)   6 inches

    D)   8 inches

    E)   10 inches

21. Which of the following mathematical expressions is equivalent to $\frac{2(x+y)}{z}$?

    A) $\frac{1}{z} \times (2x + y)$

    B) $\frac{x+y}{z} \times \frac{1}{2}$

    C) $\frac{2}{z} + \frac{x+y}{z}$

    D) $z(2x + 2y)$

    E) $\frac{2}{z} \times (x + y)$

22. Joaquin buys apples every week from the store. In April, he bought 12 apples in the first week, 15 in the second week, 10 in the third week, and 13 in the fourth week. On average, how many apples did he buy per week in April?

    A)   9.25

    B)   12.5

    C)   15

    D)   25

    E)   50

23. David has 12 chocolates to distribute among his friends. Alex got 2/3 of the chocolates. How many chocolates did he get?

    A)   2

    B)   4

    C)   8

    D)   9

    E)   10

24. If the value of y is between 0.0047 and 0.0162, which of the following could be x?

    A)   0.0005

    B)   0.0035

    C)   0.0055

    D)   0.0185

    E)   0.0238

25. The expression 3 × (2 × 43) ÷ 4 simplifies to which of the following?

A) 32

B) 64

C) 81

D) 96

E) 127

26. Use the graph below to answer the question that follows.

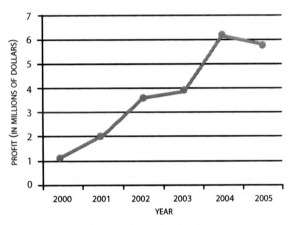

Figure 12.1. Profits by Year

According to the graph above, approximately how much did profit increase from 2003 to 2004?

A) $2.3 million

B) $3.2 million

C) $3.9 million

D) $5.0 million

E) $6.2 million

27. Use the statements below to answer the question that follows.

> The museum will offer free admission every Thursday during May and June except when:
> - A private party has reserved the museum.
> - Exhibits are closed for cleaning.

If it is a Thursday in May but the museum is not offering free admission, it must be true that:

A) a private party has reserved the museum.

B) exhibits are closed for cleaning.

C) the museum is not closed.

D) a private party has reserved the museum and exhibits are closed for cleaning.

E) a private party has reserved the museum or exhibits are closed for cleaning.

28. Use the information below to answer the question that follows.

> If Ringo has $25 dollars in his wallet, he'll pay to park in the garage.
> If Ringo has less than $25 in his wallet, he'll park on the street.
> If it's raining, Ringo will stop at the bank near his house to get $25 before he parks.

If Ringo goes downtown and parks in the garage, which of the following statements must be false?

A) Ringo left his house with less than $10 and it was raining.

B) Ringo arrived downtown with $25.

C) Ringo left his house with $25 and it was raining.

D) Ringo arrived downtown with $10.

E) Ringo arrived downtown with $25 and it was not raining.

29. A landscaping company charges 5 cents per square foot for fertilizer. How much would they charge to fertilize a 30 foot by 50 foot lawn?

A) $7.50

B) $15.00

C) $75.00

D) $150.00

E) $750.00

30. If a rectangular field has a perimeter of 44 yards and a length of 36 feet, what is the field's width?

A) 18 feet

B) 30 feet

C) 42 feet

D) 4 yards

E) 28 yards

31. The expression $(53 + 7) \times 2$ simplifies to which of the following?

A) 44

B) 139

C) 264

D) 1264

E) 1750

32. A car dealer charges 25% more for an SUV than he paid for it. If the SUV sells for $39,000, how much did the dealer spend on the car?

A) $29,250

B) $31,200

C) $32,500

D) $33,800

E) $35,000

33. Use the graph below to answer the two questions that follow.

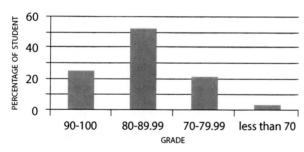

Figure 12.2. Students' Scores

For this class, a score of 70 or above is required to pass the exam. According to the graph above, what percentage of students passed this exam?

A) 3 percent

B) 18 percent

C) 56 percent

D) 69 percent

E) 97 percent

34. Grades for the exam are given out as follows:

A score below 70 is a D.
A score of 70 to 79.99 is a C.
A score of 80-89.99 is a B.
A score of 90-100 is an A.

According to the graph above, which of the following must NOT be true?

A) The fewest number of students received a C.

B) Less than half the class received an A.

C) More students received a B than any other grade.

D) More students received A's than received D's.

E) Over half the class received a C or better.

35. Use the table below to answer the question that follows.

Table 12.1 Coffee Sold

TIME OF DAY	CUPS OF COFFEE
9:00 a.m.	121
11:00 a.m.	157
1:00 p.m.	210
3:00 p.m.	245
5:00 p.m.	262

The table above shows the cumulative number of cups of coffee that a restaurant has sold at a series of time points throughout the day. How many cups of coffee were sold between 11:00 a.m. and 3:00 p.m.?

A) 17

B) 35

C) 88

D) 157

E) 245

36. A zoo pays $0.12 per pound every day to feed a 2 ton rhinoceros. How much does it cost to feed the rhinoceros every day?

A) $120

B) $240

C) $320

D) $480

E) $600

37. Melissa is ordering fencing to enclose a square area of 5625 square feet. How many feet of fencing does she need?

A) 75

B) 150

C) 300

D) 575

E) 5,625

38. If $y = 7x$, $x = 3z$, what will be the value of y if $z = 2$?

A) 40

B) 42

C) 44

D) 48

E) 50

39. Gerardo is riding his bicycle at a speed of 12 miles per hour. At 4:30 p.m. he is 54 miles from his house. If he continues riding toward his house at the same speed, how far will he be from his house at 6:00 p.m.?

A) 18 miles

B) 36 miles

C) 40 miles

D) 48 miles

E) 50 miles

40. How many 32-passenger buses will it take to carry 192 people?

A) 3

B) 5

C) 6

D) 7

E) 8

41. Read the information below; then answer the question that follows.

> The employees at a shoe store are taking an inventory. They find 210 pairs of sneakers, 177 pairs of sandals, and 185 pairs of boots. They also find 32 unlabeled boxes that each contain a pair of either sneakers, sandals, or boots.

Which of the following facts can be determined from the information given above?

A) The store has more sandals than sneakers.

B) The store has more sneakers than boots.

C) The store has more boots than sandals.

D) The store has more sandals than boots.

E) The store has more sneakers than sandals.

42. Read the information below; then answer the question that follows.

Niko starts washing dishes at 5:00 p.m. and continues washing until the end of his shift. When he stops, he's washed 660 dishes. On average, how many dishes does Niko wash in an hour?

Which single piece of additional information is required to solve this problem?

A) the time Niko's shift ended

B) the number of dishes Niko washed in the first hour of his shift

C) the number of dishes the other employees washed

D) the length of Niko's breaks

E) the number of dishes Niko washes during a typical shift

43. Solve for x.

$5x + 13 - 2x = 22$

A) $1\frac{2}{7}$

B) 3

C) 5

D) $11\frac{2}{3}$

E) 13

44. Jing wants to find 30% of 72. She does this by performing the following calculation: $\frac{30}{100} \times 72$

Which of the following methods could Jing also use to find the correct percentage?

A) 72×0.3

B) $\frac{72}{100} \times 30$

C) $\frac{72 \times 100}{30}$

D) $(72 \times 0.3) \times 100$

E) $\frac{72 \div 30}{100}$

45. Use the chart below to answer the question that follows.

Table 12.2. X and Y Relationship

X	Y
1	3
2	5
3	7
4	
5	11

The chart above displays a relationship between values of *x* and *y*. Given this relationship, what would be the value of *y* that is missing?

A) 7

B) 8

C) 9

D) 10

E) 11

46. A summary of a class's scores is shown in the table below.

Table 12.3. 9th Grade Biology Scores

AVERAGE SCORE	25TH PERCENTILE	50TH PERCENTILE	75TH PERCENTILE
80	68	84	88

According to the table above, which of the following statements is true?

A) 50% of students scored below 84.

B) 50% of students scored below 80.

C) 75% of students scored above 88.

D) The majority of students scored between 68 and 84.

E) the majority of students scored above 84.

47. Peter is going to buy notebooks and pencils at the office supply store. Notebooks are sold in packages of 3 for $5.99, and pencils are sold in packages of 20 for $2.99. Peter uses the expression below to figure out how much 12 notebooks and 100 pencils will cost.

$$\left(\frac{12}{3} \times 5.99\right) + \left(\frac{100}{20} \times 2.99\right)$$

Which of the following expressions could Peter have used instead?

A) $\frac{5.99 \times 3}{12} + \frac{2.99 \times 20}{100}$

B) $\frac{12 + 100}{5.99 + 2.99} \div (3 + 20)$

C) $(5.99 + 2.99) \times \left(\frac{12}{3} + \frac{100}{20}\right)$

D) $(5.99 + 2.99) \div \left(\frac{12}{3} + \frac{100}{20}\right)$

E) $5.99 \times 12 \div 3 + 2.99 \times 100 \div 20$

48. Which of the following mathematical statements is correct?

A) $0.0068 > 0.0081 > 0.0125$

B) $0.0125 > 0.0081 > 0.0068$

C) $0.0081 > 0.0125 > 0.0068$

D) $0.0068 > 0.0125 > 0.0081$

E) $0.0125 > 0.0068 > 0.0081$

49. Dora commutes to work every day. Her round trip times for the first week in August were 29.15 minutes, 30.75 minutes, 28.59 minutes, 27.20 minutes, and 35.62 minutes. If the times are rounded to nearest minute, what is the estimate of the total time Dora spent on her commute during this week?

A) 149

B) 150

C) 151

D) 152

E) 153

50. Based on the information above, which of the following conclusions can be made?

> The school is located 7 miles from the library.
>
> The library is located 3 miles from the theater.

A) The theater is exactly 7 miles from the school.

B) The theater is no more than 4 miles from the school.

C) The theater is no more than 10 miles from the school.

D) The theater is exactly 4 miles from the school.

E) The theater is less than 3 miles from the school.

1.	C)	26.	A)
2.	C)	27.	E)
3.	C)	28.	D)
4.	A)	29.	C)
5.	C)	30.	B)
6.	E)	31.	C)
7.	D)	32.	B)
8.	B)	33.	E)
9.	B)	34.	A)
10.	B)	35.	C)
11.	D)	36.	D)
12.	B)	37.	C)
13.	B)	38.	B)
14.	C)	39.	B)
15.	E)	40.	C)
16.	D)	41.	E)
17.	B)	42.	A)
18.	E)	43.	B)
19.	B)	44.	A)
20.	D)	45.	C)
21.	E)	46.	A)
22.	B)	47.	E)
23.	C)	48.	B)
24.	C)	49.	D)
25.	D)	50.	C)

PRACTICE TEST: WRITING

Topic 1

Oscar Wilde once said "Education is an admirable thing, but it is well to remember from time to time that nothing that is worth learning can be taught." In an essay to be read by an audience of educated adults, state whether you agree or disagree with Wilde's observation. Support your position with logical arguments and specific examples.

Topic 2

Many students find school to be a source of anxiety. Students might fear performing poorly in classes, speaking in front of groups, or being made fun of by peers. In an essay to be read by an audience of educated adults, identify a time when you felt anxious in a school environment, either as a student or a teacher, describe the situation, and explain how you handled the experience.

CPSIA information can be obtained
at www.ICGtesting.com
Printed in the USA
LVOW09s0300180417
531175LV00031B/997/P